STANDARD-ESSENTIAL PATENT HOLDERS

AVAILABILITY OF INJUNCTIVE OR EXCLUSIONARY RELIEF

LAWS AND LEGISLATION

Additional books in this series can be found on Nova's website under the Series tab.

Additional E-books in this series can be found on Nova's website under the E-book tab.

LAWS AND LEGISLATION

STANDARD-ESSENTIAL PATENT HOLDERS

AVAILABILITY OF INJUNCTIVE OR EXCLUSIONARY RELIEF

ROSADA B. VEGA
AND
MARTIN GUZMAN
EDITORS

NOVINKA

New York

For permission to use material from this book please contact us:
Telephone 631-231-7269; Fax 631-231-8175
Web Site: http://www.novapublishers.com

Library of Congress Cataloging-in-Publication Data

ISBN: 978-1-62618-207-3

Published by Nova Science Publishers, Inc. † New York

CONTENTS

PREFACE

This book provides an overview of the current debate over whether a holder of a patent essential to an industry standard, who has promised to license such patented technology on fair, reasonable, and non-discriminatory (FRAND) terms, may nevertheless obtain an injunction from a federal court or an exclusion order from the International Trade Commission against infringing products that implement the industry standard. The book first summarizes several fundamental principles of patent law, then discusses the relationship between standard-setting organizations and FRAND licensing. It continues with an explanation of the role and duties of the International Trade Commission (ITC) and how there are different legal standards that apply to the award of injunctive relief in federal courts and in the ITC. Also discussed are the recent developments relating to standard-essential patents and FRAND licensing that have occurred in federal agencies responsible for antitrust enforcement, ITC cases, and congressional hearings.

Chapter 1 - An "industry standard" is a set of technical specifications that provides a common design for a product or process. Standardization is crucial to the functioning of the modern innovation-based economy and in particular to the interoperability of technologically complex consumer electronic devices. Standards allow several firms to supply services and products that incorporate the standard, which may help to lower prices and provide greater consumer choices. Standard-setting organizations (SSOs) are voluntary membership organizations in which industry participants collaboratively select particular technical standards to be used by products in that industry.

Many SSOs require their members to adhere to licensing policies and bylaws that try to preempt the potential conflict between industry standards and patent rights; such policies generally require that members of the SSO (1) disclose patent rights that are pertinent to a proposed standard and (2) license the patented invention within a standard to others on "fair, reasonable, and nondiscriminatory" terms, a standard commonly known as "FRAND licensing."

In the past several years, there has been considerable debate over whether injunctive relief in a patent infringement lawsuit (or exclusionary relief at the International Trade Commission (ITC)) should be available to companies that own patents that cover a particular industry standard (so-called "standard-essential patent" or SEP), when those companies have previously committed themselves to license their patented technology to anyone (corporate partners or competitors) on FRAND terms. The question particularly impacts the computing and telecommunications industries, as consumer electronic products such as smartphones, GPS devices, tablets, and gaming consoles incorporate a number of industry standards that include patented technology. Many high technology companies have been involved in patent infringement lawsuits and cases before the ITC that concern disputes over SEPs and FRAND licensing. Some of the electronic device manufacturers object to what they believe are unreasonably excessive royalty requests by the SEP holder and thus do not reach an agreement to license the SEP. In such a situation, the SEP holder has sought out a judicial determination of the royalty rate or even an injunction (from federal courts) or exclusion order (from the ITC) against the sale or importation of products made by companies that did not obtain a license.

Some argue that a company that owns an SEP and that has promised to license such patent on FRAND terms essentially waives its right to seek an injunction against another company that implements the standard but fails to reach a license agreement with the SEP holder. They raise concerns about the potential negative effects on competition and U.S. consumers of allowing injunctive or exclusionary relief in cases involving FRAND-encumbered SEPs. They also believe that the threat of an injunction weighs heavily in negotiations over SEP licensing in a way that disproportionately rewards the SEP holder. However, others argue that an SEP holder is entitled to injunctive relief because an SSO's FRAND agreement does not include a promise not to seek an injunction in appropriate circumstances. Yet, they assert that if an SSO required its members to give up their right to exclude others (which is the primary right that a patent confers), participation in the voluntary standard-setting process may diminish. Furthermore, if SEP holders were limited to only damages and not injunctive relief, implementers of the industry standard may forgo negotiating a license before introducing a product and then wait for a federal court to decide on an award of damages for the infringement.

Although no legislation has been introduced in this area, the 112th Congress has demonstrated its interest in evaluating the need for possible legislative remedies by holding several hearings relating to SEPs, FRANDs, injunctive relief, and patent disputes at the ITC.

Chapter 2 - Statement of Senator Patrick Leahy, Chairman, U.S. Senate Committee on the Judiciary.

Chapter 3 - Statement of Senator Dick Durbin.

Chapter 4 - Statement of Joseph F. Wayland, Acting Assistant Attorney General, Antitrust Division, U.S. Department of Justice.

Chapter 5 - Statement of Edith Ramirez, Commissioner, Federal Trade Commission.

Chapter 6 - Section 337 of the Tariff Act of 1930 allows U.S. companies to protect themselves from imports that infringe intellectual property rights. The U.S. International Trade Commission (ITC) adjudicates complaints filed by U.S. companies alleging Section 337 violations.

Primary remedies under Section 337 include exclusion orders and cease and desist orders. In recent years, there has been an increase in the number of Section 337 proceedings or actions. Members of Congress have expressed concern about the length of time for completion of Section 337 investigations and the effectiveness of enforcement of exclusion orders.

Chapter 7 - The U.S. International Trade Commission (USITC) adjudicates allegations of unfair acts in connection with imports under Section 337 of the Tariff Act of 1930 as amended, 19 U.S.C. § 1337. Most Section 337 investigations involve allegations of infringement of patents or other IP rights. Facts and trends regarding certain aspects of Section 337 proceedings are provided within this chapter.

In: Standard-Essential Patent Holders
Editors: R. B. Vega and M. Guzman
ISBN: 978-1-62618-207-3

Chapter 1

AVAILABILITY OF INJUNCTIVE RELIEF FOR STANDARD-ESSENTIAL PATENT HOLDERS*

Brian T. Yeh

SUMMARY

An "industry standard" is a set of technical specifications that provides a common design for a product or process. Standardization is crucial to the functioning of the modern innovation-based economy and in particular to the interoperability of technologically complex consumer electronic devices. Standards allow several firms to supply services and products that incorporate the standard, which may help to lower prices and provide greater consumer choices. Standard-setting organizations (SSOs) are voluntary membership organizations in which industry participants collaboratively select particular technical standards to be used by products in that industry.

Many SSOs require their members to adhere to licensing policies and bylaws that try to preempt the potential conflict between industry standards and patent rights; such policies generally require that members of the SSO (1) disclose patent rights that are pertinent to a proposed standard and (2) license the patented invention within a standard to others on "fair, reasonable, and nondiscriminatory" terms, a standard commonly known as "FRAND licensing."

---

* This is an edited, reformatted and augmented version of a Congressional Research Service publication, CRS Report for Congress R42705, prepared for Members and Committees of Congress, from www.crs.gov, dated September 7, 2012.

In the past several years, there has been considerable debate over whether injunctive relief in a patent infringement lawsuit (or exclusionary relief at the International Trade Commission (ITC)) should be available to companies that own patents that cover a particular industry standard (so-called "standard-essential patent" or SEP), when those companies have previously committed themselves to license their patented technology to anyone (corporate partners or competitors) on FRAND terms. The question particularly impacts the computing and telecommunications industries, as consumer electronic products such as smartphones, GPS devices, tablets, and gaming consoles incorporate a number of industry standards that include patented technology. Many high technology companies have been involved in patent infringement lawsuits and cases before the ITC that concern disputes over SEPs and FRAND licensing. Some of the electronic device manufacturers object to what they believe are unreasonably excessive royalty requests by the SEP holder and thus do not reach an agreement to license the SEP. In such a situation, the SEP holder has sought out a judicial determination of the royalty rate or even an injunction (from federal courts) or exclusion order (from the ITC) against the sale or importation of products made by companies that did not obtain a license.

Some argue that a company that owns an SEP and that has promised to license such patent on FRAND terms essentially waives its right to seek an injunction against another company that implements the standard but fails to reach a license agreement with the SEP holder. They raise concerns about the potential negative effects on competition and U.S. consumers of allowing injunctive or exclusionary relief in cases involving FRAND-encumbered SEPs. They also believe that the threat of an injunction weighs heavily in negotiations over SEP licensing in a way that disproportionately rewards the SEP holder. However, others argue that an SEP holder is entitled to injunctive relief because an SSO's FRAND agreement does not include a promise not to seek an injunction in appropriate circumstances. Yet, they assert that if an SSO required its members to give up their right to exclude others (which is the primary right that a patent confers), participation in the voluntary standard-setting process may diminish. Furthermore, if SEP holders were limited to only damages and not injunctive relief, implementers of the industry standard may forgo negotiating a license before introducing a product and then wait for a federal court to decide on an award of damages for the infringement.

Although no legislation has been introduced in this area, the 112th Congress has demonstrated its interest in evaluating the need for possible legislative remedies by holding several hearings relating to SEPs, FRANDs, injunctive relief, and patent disputes at the ITC.

INTRODUCTION

This report provides on overview of the current debate over whether a holder of a patent essential to an industry standard, who has promised to license such patented technology on fair, reasonable, and non-discriminatory (FRAND) terms, may nevertheless obtain an injunction from a federal court or an exclusion order from the International Trade Commission against infringing products that implement the industry standard. The report first summarizes several fundamental principles of patent law, then discusses the relationship between standard-setting organizations and FRAND licensing. It continues with an explanation of the role and duties of the International Trade Commission (ITC) and how there are different legal standards that apply to the award of injunctive relief in federal courts and in the ITC. Finally, the report closes with an overview of recent developments relating to standard-essential patents and FRAND licensing that have occurred in federal agencies responsible for antitrust enforcement, ITC cases, and congressional hearings.

BACKGROUND

Patent Law Fundamentals

The U.S. Patent and Trademark Office (PTO) issues a patent to an inventor after PTO examiners approve the submitted patent application for an allegedly new invention.[1] An application for a patent consists of two primary parts: (1) a "specification," which is a written description of the invention enabling those skilled in the art to practice the invention, and (2) one or more claims that define the scope of the subject matter which the applicant regards as his invention.[2] Therefore, these claims define the scope of the patentee's rights under the patent.[3]

According to section 101 of the Patent Act, one who "invents or discovers any new and useful process, machine, manufacture, or any composition of matter, or any new and useful improvement thereof, may obtain a patent therefore, subject to the conditions and requirements of this title."[4] Thus, in order for an invention to qualify for patent protection, it must fall within one of the four statutory categories of patent-eligible subject matter: processes, machines, manufactures, and compositions of matter. However, the U.S. Supreme Court has articulated certain limits to § 101 of the Patent Act, stating that "laws of nature, natural phenomena, and abstract ideas" may not be patented.[5]

Before a patent may be granted, the PTO examiners must find that the new invention satisfies several substantive requirements that are set forth in the Patent Act.[6] For example, one of the statutory requirements for patentability of an invention is "novelty."[7] For an invention to be considered "novel," the subject matter must be different than, and not be wholly "anticipated" by, the so-called "prior art," or public domain materials such as publications and other patents.

Another statutory requirement is that the subject matter of an alleged invention must be "nonobvious" at the time of its creation. A patent claim is invalid if "the differences between the subject matter sought to be patented and the prior art[8] are such that the subject matter as a whole would have been obvious at the time the invention was made to a person having ordinary skill in the art to which said subject matter pertains."[9] Finally, the invention must also be "useful," which means that the invention provides a "significant and presently available," "well-defined and particular benefit to the public."[10]

The Patent Act grants patent holders the exclusive right to exclude others from making, using, offering for sale, or selling their patented invention throughout the United States, or importing the invention into the United States.[11] Whoever performs any one of these five acts during the term of the invention's patent, without the patent holder's authorization, is liable for infringement.[12]

A patent holder may file a civil action against an alleged infringer in order to enjoin him from further infringing acts (by securing an injunction, also referred to as injunctive relief).[13] The patent statute also provides federal courts with discretion to award damages to the patent holder that are "adequate to compensate for the infringement, but in no event less than a reasonable royalty for the use made of the invention by the infringer."[14] The usual term of patent protection is 20 years from the date the patent application is filed.[15] At the end of that period, others may use the invention without regard to the expired patent.

The U.S. Court of Appeals for the Federal Circuit ("Federal Circuit") is a specialized tribunal established by Congress that has exclusive appellate jurisdiction in patent cases.[16] Parties dissatisfied with the Federal Circuit's rulings may petition the U.S. Supreme Court to review the appellate court's decision.

However, the Supreme Court is not required to entertain the appeal; it has discretion to decide whether to grant certiorari to review the case.[17]

IT Industry Products and Patents

Products in the information technology (IT) industry usually incorporate many component parts that could be subject to hundreds or thousands of patents, "with no one company holding all the [patent] rights necessary to manufacture a product."[18] Commentators indicate that the IT sector is mired in what they call a "patent thicket," meaning a "dense web of overlapping [patent] rights that a company must hack its way through ... to actually commercialize new technology."[19] According to many observers, the set of potentially relevant patents for any IT product is overwhelming due to both the number of (overlapping and possibly invalid) patents *granted* in this area and the number of components *incorporated* in each product.[20]

Smartphones, tablets, and other wireless devices comprise many patented technologies that are made to comply with a large number of industry standards that relate to cellular communications, wireless Internet connectivity, and video and audio compression technology.

STANDARD-SETTING ORGANIZATIONS AND FRAND LICENSING[21]

An "industry standard" is a set of technical specifications that provides a common design for a product or process.[22] Standards sometimes arise through government action (such as the Federal Communications Commission) or through the operation of the marketplace (such as a large majority of consumers that choose one product over another). However, private industry groups called standards setting organizations (SSO) or standards developing organizations (SDO) have long been active in promulgating standards for their members. Many technology companies are members of dozens of standards bodies.[23]

Standards bodies and their members have increasingly encountered claims that a patent covers an industry standard. If the patent is valid and enforceable, it is possible that the standard cannot be employed without infringing that patent.

Industry standards potentially bring economic benefits ranging from a broad range of interoperable products to more robust, competitive markets. In turn, patent rights may promote innovation, the disclosure of new inventions and technology transfer. Conflicts between industry standards and patent rights require a careful weighing of these competing interests.

Many standards bodies have established disclosure and licensing polices to attempt to preempt the potential conflict between industry standards and patent rights. Although these policies vary, they generally require that members of the standards body (1) disclose patent rights that are pertinent to a proposed standard and (2) license the patented invention that is essential to an adopted standard to others, often on "reasonable and nondiscriminatory" terms, a standard commonly known as "RAND licensing" or "FRAND licensing" (some policies call for fair, reasonable, and nondiscriminatory terms). FRAND commitments "facilitate the bilateral licensing of patents that are needed to allow a standard to become successful and to provide assurances to implementers of the standard that the patented technologies will be available to those willing and able to license them."[24]

However, SSO policies often do not provide a specific royalty rate for a FRAND license nor do they define what would be considered "reasonable" license terms. As the Federal Trade Commission has observed, "No court has yet directly addressed the definition of FRAND, but a manufacturer that believes a patentee's license offer is unreasonable may raise the issue in a contract dispute."[25] SSO policies regarding FRAND also do not apply or bind patent holders that are not participating in the standard setting process.[26]

In the information technology (IT) industry, "products use industry standards to ensure interoperability, necessitating that manufacturers license technology that is essential to the standard."[27] Standard-essential patents (SEPs) are those patents that disclose and claim one or more inventions that are required in order to implement a particular industry standard. SEPs that are subject to a promise by the patent holder to license the technology on FRAND terms will often be referred to in this report as "FRAND-encumbered SEPs."

One federal court has explained SEPs and FRAND licensing as follows:

> Standards are important for several reasons. First, they facilitate the adoption and advancement of technology as well as the development of products that can interoperate with one another. Standards also lower costs by increasing product manufacturing volume, and they increase price competition by eliminating "switching costs" for consumers who desire to switch from products manufactured by one firm to those manufactured by another. They also lead to earlier adoption of new technology. There is, however, one downside to standards: they create "essential patents." The term "essential patents" refers to patents that are

> essential to a standard – i.e., patents that claim technologies selected by a standards development organization ("SDO"). Once a patent becomes an essential patent, it gains undue significance as a result. Companies that produce products governed by a standard become "locked in" to the technologies included in the standard. Customers have no practical choice other than to buy products that comply with the standard. Thus, the owners of essential patents gain market power. ... "FRAND commitments" are intended to prevent owners of essential patents from acquiring too much of the market power that would otherwise be inherent in owning an essential patent.[28]

Patent Hold Up

Concerns have been raised by several parties, including the U.S. Department of Justice and the Federal Trade Commission (FTC), that companies that own FRAND-encumbered SEPs may opportunistically use the threat of an injunction as leverage against other firms (colloquially referred to as a "hold up") in demanding higher royalties after the patented technology has been incorporated into an industry standard than they could have otherwise obtained had the technology not been used in the standard.[29] SEP holders could also try to use its patent to exclude a potential competitor from the U.S. market.

As recently explained in a court opinion written by federal judge Richard Posner, "[O]nce a patent becomes essential to a standard, the [SEP patent holder's] bargaining power surges because a prospective licensee has no alternative to licensing the patent; he is at the patentee's mercy."[30] Patent hold-up can also lead to other problems, such as inducing companies to delay or "avoid incorporating standardized technology in their products" and harming consumers "to the extent that companies implementing the standard pass on higher royalties in the form of a higher price."[31]

Calculating a Reasonable Royalty for a FRAND-Encumbered SEP

The FTC has stated that when a court decides to deny an injunction to a patent holder,

> the question naturally arises of what [monetary] remedy to apply. The court opinions that address the question most commonly require ongoing royalties that allow the manufacturer to continue making the infringing product. The Federal Circuit has held that this remedy can be appropriate in lieu of an injunction. ... No consensus on how to set the royalty rate has emerged from the case law, however. The Federal Circuit has stated that district courts must articulate a reasonable basis for determining the amount, and that the award should account for the changed relationship of the parties resulting from an adjudicated finding of infringement of a valid patent.[32]

Furthermore, the FTC notes that in the specific context of SEPs, "[w]hen a patentee and implementer of standardized technology bargain for a licensing rate, they do so within a framework defined by patent remedies law. That law sets the implementer's liability if negotiations break down and the parties enter patent litigation, and therefore heavily influences the negotiated amount."[33] Yet, marketplace circumstances often make the determination of an appropriate damages award in patent litigation very difficult. In some cases, the product or process that is found to infringe may incorporate numerous additional elements beyond the patented invention. In such circumstances, a court may apply "the entire market value rule," which "permits recovery of damages based upon the entire apparatus containing several features, where the patent-related feature is the basis for consumer demand."[34] On the other hand, if the court determines that the infringing sales were due to many factors beyond the use of the patented invention, the court may apply principles of "apportionment" to measure damages based upon the value of the patented feature alone.[35]

But as American University Washington College of Law Professor Jorge L. Contreras has explained, "the actual scope and contours of FRAND licenses have puzzled lawyers, regulators and courts for years, and past efforts at clarification have never been very successful."[36] He has also further described FRAND as follows:

> [T]here continues to be significant disagreement among market participants over the meaning of FRAND. This disagreement arises both in reference to the level of royalties that should be considered "reasonable," and whether other tactics, such as seeking injunctive relief, are fair game when FRAND commitments have been made. Such disagreements have serious consequences because a commitment to grant a license on FRAND terms is not itself a license. A license to operate

under a patent is not granted until the parties can agree on those "fair, reasonable and non-discriminatory" terms. So, if the parties can't agree on the terms of the FRAND license for a particular "standards-essential" patent, the frustrated licensee must either refrain from implementing the standard (and lose a significant market opportunity) or risk infringing the patent. The typical result: litigation.[37]

In a June 22, 2012, ruling by federal judge Richard Posner that dismissed with prejudice a patent infringement lawsuit between Apple and Motorola, Judge Posner offered his guidance to courts on how to calculate an appropriate royalty for a FRAND-encumbered SEP:

> The proper method of computing a FRAND royalty starts with what the cost to the licensee would have been of obtaining, just before the patented invention was declared essential to compliance with the industry standard, a license for the function performed by the patent. That cost would be a measure of the value of the patent qua patent. ... The purpose of the FRAND requirements ... is to confine the patentee's royalty demand to the value conferred by the patent itself as distinct from the additional value—the hold-up value—conferred by the patent's being designated as standard-essential.[38]

In a July 18, 2012, letter from Apple to Senators Leahy and Grassley (the Chairman and Ranking Member of the Senate Judiciary Committee, respectively), Apple offered its opinion on the proper determination of FRAND royalties:

> [I]t is wrong to charge FRAND royalties on the end price of a device like the iPhone, whose value arises more from product-differentiating technology than standardized technology, and whose price reflects this. A FRAND royalty on an iPhone should be no higher than a FRAND royalty on any other 3G phone. It is akin to a toll on a highway: the toll is identical for a jalopy and a new sports car—the sports car does not pay more just because it is faster, more stylish, and has a better sound system. Nor is it FRAND to seek royalties based on the mere fact that a particular technology was standardized; a FRAND royalty should be limited to the true technical value of a patented technology, not the artificially inflated value based on the fact that it has been included in a mandatory industry standard.[39]

INTERNATIONAL TRADE COMMISSION

Besides seeking legal relief for infringement in the federal courts, U.S. patent holders may also obtain an order from the U.S. International Trade Commission (ITC or Commission) preventing the importation of foreign goods that infringe their rights. The ITC is an independent,

nonpartisan, quasi-judicial federal government agency responsible for investigating and arbitrating complaints of violations of section 337 of the Tariff Act of 1930 (19 U.S.C. § 1337), which prohibits unfair methods of competition or other unfair acts in the importation of products into the United States. Section 337 also prohibits the importation of articles that infringe valid U.S. patents, copyrights, processes, trademarks, or protected design rights. (The majority of unfair competition acts asserted under section 337 involve allegations of patent infringement.[40]) However, a patent holder must satisfy section 337's "domestic industry" requirement in order for the ITC to adjudicate a patent dispute. That is, section 337 declares unlawful the importation into the United States of articles that infringe a U.S. intellectual property right, but *only if* "an industry in the United States, relating to the articles protected by the patent, copyright, trademark, mask work, or design concerned, exists or is in the process of being established."[41] As the Federal Circuit has explained, Congress included the domestic industry requirement because it "recognized that the Commission is fundamentally a trade forum, not an intellectual property forum, and that only those intellectual property owners who are actively engaged in steps leading to the exploitation of the intellectual property should have access to the Commission."[42] A patent holder can satisfy the domestic industry requirement by showing one of the following:

1. significant investment in plant and equipment;
2. significant employment of labor or capital; or
3. substantial investment in its exploitation, including engineering, research and development, or licensing.[43]

Congress added the third provision listed above in 1988[44] in order to help more companies satisfy the domestic industry requirement, including those that lack manufacturing activities but instead engage in licensing and research.[45] The ITC has *in rem* jurisdiction over accused imported products, and the ITC need not have personal jurisdiction over accused manufacturers or meet venue requirements.[46]

The ITC's Administrative Law Judges (ALJs) manage litigation, preside over evidentiary hearings, and make an initial determination (ID) in the agency's investigations involving unfair practices in import trade.

The ID as to whether Section 337 has been violated is certified to the Commission (a six-member decision-making body that heads the ITC); the Commission may then review and adopt, modify, or reverse the ALJ's ID; if the Commission declines to review the ID, then the ID becomes the determination of the Commission.[47]

The Commission's determination is sent to the President; he may veto such determination "for policy reasons" within a 60-day review period.[48] If the President notifies the Commission of his disapproval of the determination, the determination "shall have no force or effect."[49]

If the President does not veto the determination within the 60-day review period, the determination becomes final on the day after the close of the period, or the day on which the President expressly notifies the Commission of his approval.[50]

Anyone adversely affected by a decision of the ITC may appeal the decision, within 60 day after the determination becomes final, to the Federal Circuit.[51] The agency's decisions are reviewed in accordance with the standards of judicial deference provided by the Administrative Procedure Act.[52]

The largely deferential review standards provide that the court shall uphold the agency's factual findings when the court determines that they are supported by substantial evidence[53] on the record as a whole, and that the agency's action is not arbitrary, capricious, an abuse of discretion, or otherwise not in accordance with law.

However, the Federal Circuit has held that the construction and interpretation of patent claims are a matter of law that receive de novo review by a reviewing court.[54] In addition, federal district courts do not give *res judicata* or collateral estoppel effect to ITC decisions; thus, patent holders that win a case before the ITC must relitigate the issue of patent infringement liability before the federal courts.[55]

The ITC has the power to order several forms of prospective injunctive relief, including ordering the U.S. Customs and Border Protection (CBP) to stop imports from entering U.S. borders (an exclusion order), or issuing cease and desist orders that prohibit parties from distributing or selling infringing articles from existing U.S. inventory. However, unlike the federal courts, the ITC lacks the statutory authority to award monetary damages for patent infringement (past or future).[56]

INJUNCTIVE RELIEF IN THE FEDERAL COURTS AND AT THE ITC: APPLICABLE STANDARDS

Standards for Injunctive Relief in the Federal Courts

To prevent the violation of any right secured by a patent, the Patent Act provides that a federal court "may grant injunctions in accordance with the principles of equity ... on such terms as the court deems reasonable."[57] An injunction prevents the adjudicated infringer from practicing the patented invention until the patent expires. Without the right to obtain injunctive relief, "the right to exclude granted to the patentee would have only a fraction of the value it was intended to have, and would no longer be as great an incentive to engage in the toils of scientific and technological research."[58]

In practice, for much of its history the U.S. Court of Appeals for the Federal Circuit routinely granted injunctions to patent owners that prevailed in infringement litigation, in keeping with its opinion that "[b]ecause the right to exclude recognized in a patent is but the essence of the concept of property, the general rule is that a permanent injunction will issue once infringement and validity have been adjudged."[59] However, the U.S. Supreme Court in its May 2006 opinion, *eBay v. MercExchange,*[60] unanimously vacated the Federal Circuit's "general rule" calling for a permanent injunction upon a finding of patent infringement. Writing for the Court, Justice Clarence Thomas explained that traditional principles of equity that govern issuance of injunctive relief "apply with equal force to disputes arising under the Patent Act."[61] Thus, in order for a court to grant injunctive relief, a plaintiff must satisfy a four-factor test by demonstrating:

1. that it has suffered an irreparable injury;
2. that remedies available at law, such as monetary damages, are inadequate to compensate for that injury;
3. that, considering the balance of hardships between the plaintiff and defendant, a remedy in equity is warranted; and
4. that the public interest would not be disserved by a permanent injunction.[62]

Two concurring opinions, written by Chief Justice John Roberts, Jr., and Justice Anthony Kennedy, were filed in *eBay* and reveal an apparent disagreement among the justices. Chief Justice Roberts' concurring opinion, joined by Justices Antonin Scalia and Ruth Bader Ginsburg, predicted that injunctive relief will likely continue to be the usual remedy for patent infringement, consistent with the "long tradition of equity practice."[63] A district court's equitable discretion in granting or denying an injunction in patent cases, therefore, is not unfettered, in the view of these three Justices.

While agreeing with Chief Justice Robert's concurrence that "history may be instructive" in applying the traditional four-factor test for deciding whether an injunction should issue or not in patent infringement cases, Justice Kennedy's concurring opinion, joined by Justices John Paul Stevens, David Souter, and Stephen Breyer, suggested that historical practice might not necessarily be helpful for courts to follow when dealing with some patent infringement suits in the current business environment: "[T]rial courts should bear in mind that in many instances the nature of the patent being enforced and the economic function of the patent holder present considerations quite unlike earlier cases."[64] Justice Kennedy acknowledged the emergence of patent holding companies (so-called "patent trolls")[65] and their impact on patent litigation today:

> An industry has developed in which firms use patents not as a basis for producing and selling goods but, instead, primarily for obtaining licensing fees.... For these firms, an injunction, and the potentially serious sanctions arising from its violation, can be employed as a bargaining tool to charge exorbitant fees to companies that seek to buy licenses to practice the patent.... When the patented invention is but a small component of the product the companies seek to produce and the threat of an injunction is employed simply for undue leverage in negotiations, legal damages may well be sufficient to compensate for the infringement and an injunction may not serve the public interest.[66]

The *eBay* case "represented a sea change in patent litigation" and helped reduce the problem of patent holdup.[67] Before *eBay*, "[p]atentees who owned rights in very small pieces of complex, multi-component products could threaten to shut down the entire product. As a result, even a very weak patent could command a high royalty in settlement from defendants afraid of gambling their entire product on a jury's decision."[68] However, in following Justice Kennedy's concurrence in *eBay,* federal courts have rarely issued injunctions to patent holding companies.[69] In addition, *eBay* has impacted the availability of injunctive relief for SEP holders that promised to license on FRAND terms. The Commissioner of the FTC has observed that because federal courts must apply the *eBay* equitable analysis in deciding whether to grant injunctive relief, "it may be difficult for RAND-encumbered SEP holders to show that money damages are inadequate because they have already committed to license their intellectual property on RAND terms."[70] In the recent patent infringement lawsuit between Apple and Motorola that Judge Posner dismissed, he opined:

> To begin with Motorola's injunctive claim, I don't see how, given FRAND, I would be justified in enjoining Apple from infringing the '898 unless Apple refuses to pay a royalty that meets the FRAND requirement. By committing to license its patents on FRAND terms, Motorola committed to license the '898 to anyone willing to pay a FRAND royalty and thus implicitly acknowledged that a royalty is adequate compensation for a license to use that patent. How could it do otherwise? How could it be permitted to enjoin Apple from using an invention that it contends Apple *must* use if it wants to make a cell phone with UMTS telecommunications capability—without which it would not be a cell *phone*.[71]

Standards for Exclusionary Relief in the ITC

As an administrative agency and not an Article III court, the ITC has asserted that the Supreme Court's *eBay* decision does *not* apply to ITC remedy determinations under section 337; thus, the ITC is not required to apply the traditional four-factor test for injunctive relief used by federal district courts. This position was upheld by the Federal Circuit in its December 2010 opinion, *Spansion, Inc. v. ITC*.[72] According to the Federal Circuit:

> The legislative history of the amendments to Section 337 indicates that Congress intended injunctive relief to be the normal remedy for a Section 337 violation and that a showing of irreparable harm is not required to receive such injunctive relief. This is shown by two distinct actions of Congress. First, in passing the Tariff Act of 1930, Pub. L. No. 71-361, 46 Stat. 590, Congress eliminated the monetary remedy for intellectual property import violations, representing a legislative determination that an injunction is the only available remedy for violations of Section 337. Second, in 1988, Congress amended Section 337 by passing the Omnibus Trade and Competitiveness Act of 1988, P.L. 100-418, 102 Stat. 1107, explicitly removing the requirement of

proof of injury to the domestic industry and making it unnecessary to show irreparable harm to the patentee in the case of infringement by importation.

As contrasted with the remedial scheme established by Congress for proceedings before the Commission, the statutory remedies available in proceedings before the district courts are quite different. In addition to the remedy of damages under 35 U.S.C. § 284, Congress gave district courts the discretion to grant injunctive relief and in doing so made explicit that such discretion is to be exercised "in accordance with the principles of equity ... on such terms as the court deems reasonable."[73]

Section 337 of the Tariff Act of 1930 permits the ITC, in deciding whether to issue an exclusion order, to consider the effect of such exclusion upon:

1. the public health and welfare,
2. competitive conditions in the United States economy,
3. the production of like or directly competitive articles in the United States, and
4. United States consumers.[74]

Law professors Colleen Chien and Mark Lemley note that although the ITC appears to have sufficient statutory authority to take into account a variety of public interest factors (including consumers and competition) when deciding whether to grant an exclusion order, the ITC rarely has exercised that power.[75] The ITC has refrained from imposing an exclusion order based on these considerations on only three previous occasions, and none in the past quarter century. These cases, however, involved products that are important to human health or other critical national policy goal, including "car parts necessary for improved fuel efficiency, scientific equipment for nuclear physics research, and hospital burn beds." [76] The law professors surmise that the reason the ITC rarely finds that an exclusion order would threaten the public interest is because "the ITC views enforcing patents as in the public interest, with the result that the public interest analyst starts out with a thumb on the scale in favor of the patentee."[77]

The Federal Trade Commission (FTC) has observed that "unlike the situation in district court, a finding of infringement in the ITC leads to a nearly automatic exclusion order."[78] Thus, the FTC explained that some parties are "worried that patentees might bring suit in the ITC more frequently in the future in the hope of obtaining exclusion orders in circumstances where injunctions might not have been granted in federal district court."[79] Law professors Chien and Lemley argue that in the aftermath of *eBay,* patent assertion entities (so-called "patent trolls") "are flocking to the ITC" in search of an injunction or the threat of one.[80] However, in June 2012, the ITC published an analysis of its caseload data that it claims does not support the suggestion that *eBay* has greatly contributed to an increase in complaint filings by patent trolls at the ITC.[81]

Law professors Chien and Lemley have noted that "[l]egislative and judicial improvements made to patent law procedures and remedies simply don't apply in the ITC,"[82] citing the *eBay* example as well as the recently enacted Leahy-Smith America Invents Act of 2011 (AIA). The AIA restricts the ability of plaintiffs to sue multiple unrelated defendants for infringement in the same case or same trial "based solely on allegations that they each have infringed the patent or patents in suit," [83] which is a common practice among patent assertion entities ("patent trolls"). However, Congress did not extend this joinder limitation to the ITC, the law professors observed. Thus, "[w]hile the number of defendants per case declined in the district court immediately following passage of the [AIA], it has stayed steady in the ITC."[84]

Recent Developments Relating to Standard-Essential Patents and FRAND Licensing

The question arises, and has been the subject of much debate in federal courts, government agencies, scholarly publications, mass media, and congressional hearings, whether the incorporation of a patent into an industry standard should be regarded as limiting the SEP holder's ability to obtain injunctive or exclusionary relief from federal courts and the ITC against alleged infringers. Few would disagree that the SEP holder should be entitled to monetary damages in a situation where an SEP holder offers a FRAND license to an implementer of a standard, but the implementer (believing that the proposed royalty rates are too excessive) refuses to license the SEP and produces the infringing product anyway. However, in such a situation, is injunctive or exclusionary relief appropriate for the SEP holder against any party that wants to practice the standard but does not agree to the SEP holder's licensing terms? The debate on this question generally centers around the "appropriateness" of such relief—those who favor limiting injunctions in this situation would like to see injunctive relief rarely awarded to an SEP holder unless there were extraordinary circumstances.[85] On the other side of the debate are those who oppose a diminishment of the patent holder's right to exclude others from making, using, or selling a patented invention without the patent holder's express authorization, fearing that it would "tip the balance in favor of infringers to the detriment of innovation and ultimately consumers."[86]

U.S. Department of Justice Antitrust Division's Review of Patent Portfolio Acquisitions

The U.S. Justice Department Antitrust Division has noted that the recent acquisitions in 2011 of substantial patent portfolios by prominent technology companies (Google, Apple, and Microsoft) which include SEPs "highlight the complex intersection of intellectual property rights and antitrust law and the need to determine the correct balance between the rightful exercise of patent rights and a patent holder's incentive and ability to harm competition through the anticompetitive use of those rights."[87] A partnership that included Apple and Microsoft purchased 6,000 patents from Nortel Networks in a June 2011 bankruptcy auction, many of which covered wireless communication standards and to which that Nortel had committed to license on FRAND terms. Google entered into an agreement in August 2011 to acquire Motorola Mobility, which holds 17,000 patents, several hundreds of which pertain to wireless Internet and cellular communication standards and to which Motorola Mobility had committed to license on FRAND terms.

The Antitrust Division of the Justice Department approved the acquisition of these patent portfolios because it believed that "neither acquisition was likely to substantially lessen competition for wireless devices."[88] Furthermore, the Division was reassured by these companies' public commitments to adhere to FRAND licenses, which are excerpted below:

> Microsoft: "Industry standards are vitally important to the development of the Internet and to interoperability among mobile devices and other computers. The international standards system works well because firms that contribute to standards promise to make their essential patents available to others on fair, reasonable and nondiscriminatory terms. Consumers and the entire industry will suffer if, in disregard of this promise, firms seek to block others from shipping products on the basis of such standard essential patents."[89]

> Apple: "A party who made a FRAND commitment to license its cellular standards essential patents or otherwise acquired assets/rights from a party who made the FRAND commitment must not seek injunctive relief on such patents. Seeking an injunction would be a violation of the party's commitment to FRAND licensing."[90]

The Antitrust Division noted that Google's commitment to FRAND is not as straightforward as Apple's and Microsoft's, explaining that "Google has stated ... that its policy is to refrain from seeking injunctive relief for the infringement of SEPs against a counter-party, but apparently only for disputes involving future license revenues, and only if the counterparty: forgoes certain defenses such as challenging the validity of the patent; pays the full disputed amount into escrow; and agrees to a reciprocal process regarding injunctions."[91] Thus, in the Antitrust Division's view, Google "does not directly provide the same assurance as the other companies' statements concerning the exercise of its newly acquired patent rights."[92]

Nevertheless, the Antitrust Division concluded, "[i]f adhered to in practice, these positions could significantly reduce the possibility of a [patent] hold up or use of an injunction as a threat to inhibit or preclude innovation and competition."[93]

Recent Cases Before the ITC Involving Standard-Essential Patents

Several cases before the ITC involve whether a FRAND-encumbered SEP holder is entitled to exclusionary relief.

In the Matter of Certain Gaming and Entertainment Consoles, Related Software, and Components Thereof

The ITC is currently investigating a case involving Motorola Mobility's claims of patent infringement against Microsoft's Xbox 360 gaming console; at issue is whether to grant an exclusion order in favor of Motorola Mobility,[94] a holder of standard-essential patents relating to video transmission and compression and wireless connectivity, that has previously agreed to license its technologies on FRAND terms and yet has not reached an agreement with Microsoft on reasonable license terms.[95] In May 2012, the ALJ assigned to the case recommended a ban on the importation of Xbox consoles[96] after he had made an earlier determination that the device infringed four patents owned by Motorola.[97]

In the wake of the ALJ's initial determination in the Xbox case, several Members of Congress submitted letters to the Chairman of the ITC to express their concerns over the potential exclusionary order against the gaming console, while other Members have urged the ITC to protect Motorola's patent rights.[98] A June 7, 2012 letter from the House Judiciary Committee to the ITC signed by Representatives Lamar Smith, John Conyers, and Melvin Watt, argued that:

> A party making a RAND commitment for SEPs promises not to deny a license to anyone who implements the standard. Patent owners agree that they will seek reasonable royalties and not pursue a court order or an exclusion order to prevent the importation or sale of an implementer's product. The aims underlying RAND arrangements may be undermined when a patent owner either petitions the Commission for an exclusion order or makes an unreasonable royalty demand. ...
>
> In our view, a failure to honor a RAND commitment undermines confidence in the standards system and disrupts competition and innovation. If companies refuse to comply with their RAND commitments and instead treat their SEPs as a weapon to block others from distributing products that implement key standards, they will prevent and inhibit innovation and competition. Ultimately, this behavior threatens to disrupt competition and undermines the creation and adoption of standards that are at the heart of modern communications technologies and the digital networks that are critical to the global economy. Technological innovation, predictable and stable commerce, and strong competition may be harmed by inappropriate assertions of SEP rights through exclusion orders.[99]

Several Members of Congress from Illinois, where Motorola is based, wrote in their letter to the ITC:

> We strongly support vigorous intellectual property right protection, including injunctive and exclusionary relief, that appropriates and reasonably rewards past innovation and encourages new development, which has been and must continue to be the foundation of this country's economic success. Indeed, to maintain a level playing field in circumstances in which entities are found to be infringing U.S. intellectual property rights but will not provide reasonable compensation to the owner and developer of these rights, injunctive and exclusionary relief must be available and rigorously enforced. Denying legitimate

patent protection adversely affects domestic commerce and business in a very meaningful way by preventing domestic companies from protecting their innovations, and thus discouraging domestic companies from investing in future innovation.[100]

A June 19, 2012 letter to the ITC from Senators Herb Kohl, Mike Lee, Jon Kyl, John Cornyn, Jim Risch, and John Hoeven urged the ITC to consider the public interest arguments carefully in cases in which SEPs are at issue:

> Any precedent that would enable or encourage companies to include their patented technology in a standard, commit to license included patents on RAND terms, and then seek to secure an exclusion order despite a breach of that commitment would thus implicate significant policy concerns. Such an outcome would severely undermine broad participation in the standards-setting process, which would in turn threaten the meaningful benefits these standards provide for both industries and consumers.[101]

On June 29, 2012, the Commission ordered a remand of the Xbox investigation to the ALJ with instructions for the ALJ to apply newly issued Commission opinions that some observers predict may change the ALJ's determination in favor of Microsoft.[102] In any case, the remand to the ALJ will cause significant delay in the case, with a target date for the final decision being set as July 23, 2013.[103]

In the Matter of Certain Wireless Communications Devices, Portable Music and Data Processing Devices, Computers, and Components Thereof

At issue in this investigation by the ITC is whether Apple infringes certain patents pertaining to 3G wireless technology that are held by Motorola Mobility with its importation into the United States and sale within the United States of iPhone and iPad devices. The ALJ made an initial determination in April 2012 that Apple infringed one of Motorola's patents, which is a FRANDencumbered SEP.[104]

On June 25, 2012, the Commission provided notice that it was planning on reviewing the ALJ's initial determination and requested written submissions from parties (and non-parties) on several questions relating to FRAND, including:

1. If the record of an investigation lacks evidence sufficient to support a RAND-based affirmative defense (e.g., equitable estoppel, implied license, waiver, etc.), under what circumstances (if any) should a RAND obligation nonetheless preclude issuance of an exclusion order?
2. Does the mere existence of a RAND obligation preclude issuance of an exclusion order?
3. Should a patent owner that has refused to offer a license to a named respondent in a Commission investigation on a RAND obligated patent be able to obtain an exclusion order?
4. Should a patent owner that has refused to negotiate a license on RAND terms with a named respondent in a Commission investigation be precluded from obtaining an exclusion order?
5. Should a patent owner who has offered a RAND license that the named respondent in a Commission investigation has rejected be precluded from obtaining an exclusion order?[105]

The FTC submitted a statement to the ITC that sets forth the potential economic and competitive impact of injunctive relief on disputes involving SEPs:

> ITC issuance of an exclusion or cease and desist order in matters involving RAND-encumbered SEPs, where infringement is based on implementation of standardized technology, has the potential to cause substantial harm to U.S. competition, consumers, and innovation. ... [W]e are concerned that a patentee can make a RAND commitment as part of the standard setting process, and then seek an exclusion order for infringement of the RAND-encumbered SEP as a way of securing royalties that may be inconsistent with that RAND commitment.[106]

A submission to the ITC by 19 economics and law professors argued that "ITC exclusion orders generally should not be granted under § 1337(d)(1) on the basis of patents subject to obligations to license on 'reasonable and non-discriminatory' (RAND) terms" because such an exclusion "would undermine the significant pro-competitive and pro-consumer benefits that RAND promises produce and the investments they enable." [107] The submission contends that "[t]hrough their promises [to license on FRAND terms], [SEP] patent holders have traded the right to exclude for the privilege of being declared essential to the standard."[108] However, the professors recognized that an exception to this general rule might be if "district court jurisdiction is lacking, the patent is valid and infringed, and the public interest favors issuing an exclusion order."[109]

On August 24, 2012, the Commission reversed the ALJ's determination that Apple infringed Motorola's SEP.[110] The decision, however, does not discuss the Commission's position on the questions it posed to the parties relating to FRAND and whether an exclusion order is appropriate in cases involving SEPs.

HEARINGS IN THE 112TH CONGRESS

In June and July 2012, Congress held several oversight hearings that examined the issue of SEPs and the ITC.

June 20, 2012, Senate Judiciary Committee

The U.S. Patent and Trademark Office Director David Kappos offered his views on standard-essential patents in response to questions posed by Senators Patrick Leahy and Mike Lee in a Senate Judiciary Committee hearing held on June 20, 2012.[111]

Senator Leahy asked Director Kappos whether holders of SEPs that seek an exclusion order from the ITC after previously committing to FRAND licensing could have anti-competitive effects. Director Kappos stated that the situation is "cause for careful study," but nevertheless he stated that pledges by competitors to adhere to FRAND must be kept. Yet, he also emphasized that a FRAND commitment does not stand for licensing under any terms and conditions.

Furthermore, he argued that FRAND should not eliminate all opportunities to enforce a patent because then no company will have any incentive to take a license for the patented technology in the first place. In response to a question posed by Senator Lee, Director Kappos further expressed his concerns about the use of exclusion orders in SEP cases before the ITC. But he noted that there is a need to find a proper balance that is beneficial to both patent owners and those that engage in standard setting.

On July 10, 2012, Google sent a letter to Senators Leahy and Grassley in which it urged caution in taking any steps to change the status quo in the area of FRAND-encumbered SEPs:

Google agrees that courts and the International Trade Commission (the "ITC") may consider whether a patentee has complied with its licensing obligation as a relevant factor in determining whether the public interest supports awarding exclusionary relief based on a standard-essential patent ("SEP"). ... But at the same time, courts and regulators must avoid the temptation to adopt categorical rules that deprive patentees of the rights that Congress and the Patent Office conferred on them and that the patentees did not intend to relinquish through their FRAND licensing promises."[112]

July 11, 2012, Senate Judiciary Committee

The Senate Judiciary Committee held a hearing on July 11, 2012 with the title, "Oversight of the Impact on Competition of Exclusion Orders to Enforce Standards-Essential Patents." The hearing had two witnesses, Joseph Wayland, the Acting Assistant Attorney General, Antitrust Division of the U.S. Department of Justice, and Edith Ramirez, the Commissioner of the Federal Trade Commission. Acting Assistant Attorney General Wayland noted that in the Antitrust Division's review of the 2011 patent portfolio acquisitions by the major technology companies, it "investigated whether patent acquisitions would change the incentives or abilities of the new owners to obtain higher royalties from their competitors, particularly by using the threat of an injunction or exclusion order."[113] In addition, he revealed that the Antitrust Division has "continued closely to monitor the use of F/RAND-encumbered standard-essential patents in the wireless device industry, particularly as they relate to smartphones and computer tablets, to ensure that they do not stifle competition and innovation in this important industry.[114] Commissioner Ramirez stated that SSO members do not typically negotiate licenses for SEPs *before* a standard is adopted, but rather require SEP owners to agree to license SEPs on FRAND terms "as a *quid pro quo* for the inclusion of their patents in a standard."[115] She observed, however, that while "[t]his [practice] makes it easier to adopt a standard, [it] also creates the potential for hold-up because it defers the negotiation on price until after the standard is adopted."[116] Commissioner Ramirez argued that the injunctive relief for a FRAND-encumbered SEP holder is likely inappropriate in most cases:

"A royalty negotiation that occurs under threat of an injunction or an exclusion order may be weighted heavily in favor of the patent holder in a way that is in tension with the RAND commitment. High switching costs combined with the threat of an exclusion order could allow a patent holder to obtain unreasonable licensing terms despite its RAND commitment, whether or not the invention is highly valuable on its own, because implementers are locked into practicing the standard. This is an even bigger problem when the hold-up creates a very high cost for a very small component of the overall product. In these ways, the threat of injunctive relief, including an exclusion order, may allow the holder of a RAND-encumbered SEP to realize royalty rates that reflect patent hold-up, rather than the value of the patent relative to alternatives. This can raise prices to consumers, distort incentives to innovate, and undermine the standard setting process."[117]

Finally, Commissioner Ramirez asserted that the ITC possesses sufficient statutory authority to limit the possibility of hold-up under its obligation to consider several public interest factors before deciding whether to grant an exclusion order to an FRAND-encumbered SEP holder that has not complied with its FRAND obligation. However, she offered that if "the ITC finds that its public interest authority is not flexible enough to allow this analysis, then Congress should consider whether it should amend Section 337 to give the ITC more flexible authority to prevent hold-up."[118]

July 18, 2012, House Judiciary Subcommittee on Intellectual Property, Competition and the Internet

The House Judiciary Subcommittee on Intellectual Property, Competition and the Internet held a hearing on July 18, 2012, entitled "The International Trade Commission and Patent Disputes." Witnesses included Professor Colleen Chien of Santa Clara University School of Law as well as general counsels from several U.S. companies. Unlike the July 11th Senate Judiciary Committee hearing on SEPs and the ITC, this hearing focused primarily on the impact of non-practicing entities (which include "patent trolls") on the ITC's docket; however, the topic of SEPs was discussed by some of the witnesses. First, Professor Chien explained that "now that most technology products are manufactured abroad and Congress has relaxed the domestic industry requirement [in 1988], nearly every patentee is a potential ITC complainant and nearly every patent defendant is a potential ITC respondent."[119] Furthermore, because many patent holders in the high technology industry are filing complaints with the ITC in the hopes of obtaining injunctive relief that is more difficult to find in federal courts, this litigious behavior "undoes the progress that *eBay* represents, and it contributes to the favorable climate for patent trolling and holdup present in today's patent system."[120] Finally, she suggested that the ITC could change the way it issues exclusion orders in a way that "minimizes disruption to consumers and the holdup to manufacturers;" for example, the ITC could carefully tailor the scope of the injunction and also delay the effective date of an injunction in order to give time to the infringer to "design around" the patent (if that is a feasible option).[121] However, "designing around" a patent may not be possible in the case of a SEP because doing so may mean that the product does not comply with the standard:

> Critically, SEPs cannot, by definition, be designed around without sacrificing compliance with the standard. This makes them different than non-SEP patents that, if they cover minor features, can be designed around without sacrificing key functionality. While inventing around does not eliminate the danger of patent hold-up, it does provide a check on the bargaining power wielded by patent holders that seek injunctive relief. This check is much weaker when the patents are standards-essential. There, disabling even a single feature to avoid infringement of an SEP can greatly detract from the value of a product by making it inoperable for its intended purpose, for example, a laptop that cannot connect to a Wi-Fi network. Furthermore, many consumers, counting on standards to provide the functionality they require, are unwilling to purchase noncompliant products. An exclusion order that forces manufacturers to produce noncompliant products would undermine the network effects associated with successful standards and harm consumers.[122]

Albert Foer, president of the American Antitrust Institute (AAI), testified that:

> Although it is not feasible to establish perfect rules on what price for licensing a SEP would be fair and reasonable, some minimal standards are appropriate. The AAI agrees with the FTC's promotion of two principles. First, the determination should rest on ex ante incremental value rather than ex post total market value. Second, the royalty base should be the smallest affected component rather than the entire device. Because FRAND commitments are today so generally vague that they do

not provide adequate protection against holdup conduct, SSOs should be required to move in the direction of ex ante disclosure of proposed or maximum license terms.[123]

Furthermore, Mr. Foer argued that "[a]n injunction is not an appropriate remedy for SEP infringement as a matter of both good law and good policy" and that "SSO rules should make clear that the provider of a FRAND commitment in the course of a standard development proceeding waives any right to seek either injunctive relief in court or an exclusion order at the International Trade Commission."[124]

Bernard Cassidy, General Counsel of Tessera Technologies, Inc., urged Congress not to make any changes to Section 337 that would weaken the ITC's jurisdiction or powers, because doing so, he claimed, "would benefit foreign economies, foreign competitors, and other foreign manufacturers to the detriment of the U.S. economy."[125] He also rejected arguments by some commentators that Congress apply the *eBay* case to the ITC because "[g]iven that the only remedy available to the ITC is exclusion orders, mandating application of *eBay* would substantially weaken the power of the ITC to deal with unfair trade practices."[126] Finally, he predicted that reducing or eliminating the availability of exclusion orders or injunctions for FRAND-encumbered SEP holders would mean that "fewer innovators would participate in SSOs with such IPR rules (or make FRAND commitments if they do participate) or engage in R&D for technologies that may be standardized. Reduced participation in SSOs or reduced funding of R&D would likely result in delay, technologically inferior standards, and reduced information about patents implicated by standards."[127]

In an August 2, 2012 letter sent by the American Intellectual Property Law Association (AIPLA) to Congressmen Bob Goodlatte and Mel Watt (the Chairman and Ranking Member of the House Judiciary Subcommittee on Intellectual Property, Competition and the Internet, respectively), AIPLA argued against the application of the *eBay* rule for ITC proceedings and expressed several concerns about proposals to categorically deny injunctive or exclusionary relief to SEP holders:

> Like all patent owners, SEP owners should have the right to protect their intellectual property from infringement. Removing this patent enforcement option at the ITC may be harmful to the rapidly growing IT and telecommunications industries that often participate in the SSOs. Additionally, a categorical exclusion of SEPs from Section 337

proceedings would make it easier for foreign companies to import infringing goods into the U.S.[128]

End Notes

[1] 35 U.S.C. § 131.
[2] 35 U.S.C. § 112.
[3] 3-8 DONALD S. CHISUM, CHISUM ON PATENTS § 8.01 (2006).
[4] 35 U.S.C. § 101.
[5] Diamond v. Diehr, 450 U.S. 175, 185 (1981).
[6] 35 U.S.C. §§ 102, 103(a).
[7] 35 U.S.C. § 102.
[8] "Prior art" is a legal term of art that refers to the materials (usually called "references" in patent law) that comprise the available knowledge regarding the subject matter of the invention sought to be patented, such as other issued patents, publications, and evidence of actual uses or sales of the technology. ROGER SCHECHTER & JOHN THOMAS, PRINCIPLES OF PATENT LAW 4-1 (2d ed. 2004).
[9] 35 U.S.C. § 103(a).
[10] In re Fischer, 421 F.3d 1365, 1371 (Fed. Cir. 2005).
[11] 35 U.S.C. §§ 154(a)(1), 271(a).
[12] 35 U.S.C. § 271(a).
[13] 35 U.S.C. § 283.
[14] 35 U.S.C. § 284.
[15] 35 U.S.C. §154(a)(2).
[16] 28 U.S.C. § 1295(a)(1).
[17] 28 U.S.C. § 1254(1).
[18] Federal Trade Commission, The Evolving IP Marketplace (March 2011), available at http://www.ftc.gov/os/2011/03/ 110307patentreport.pdf, at 221 (hereinafter "FTC Report").
[19] Carl Shapiro, Navigating the Patent Thicket: Cross Licenses, Patent Pools, and Standard Setting, in INNOVATION POLICY AND THE ECONOMY 119, 125 (2001).
[20] JAMES BESSEN AND MICHAEL J. MEURER, PATENT FAILURE 8 (2008).
[21] Portions of this section of the memorandum have been borrowed and adapted from an earlier CRS report that examines the potential conflicts between industry standards and intellectual property, see CRS Report RL31951, Innovation, Intellectual Property, and Industry Standards, by John R. Thomas.
[22] Mark A. Lemley, "Intellectual Property Rights and Standard-Setting Organizations," 90 CALIFORNIA LAW REVIEW (2002), at 1889.
[23] Id. at 1907.
[24] Oversight of the Impact on Competition of Exclusion Orders to Enforce Standard-Essential Patents: Hearing Before the Senate Judiciary Committee, 112th Cong., 2d Sess., July 11, 2012 (statement of Joseph F. Wayland, Acting Assistant Attorney General, Antitrust Division, U.S. Department of Justice), at 5 (hereinafter "SEP Hearing").
[25] FTC Report, supra note 18, at 194.
[26] Id. at 192-93.
[27] Id.

[28] Research in Motion Ltd. v. Motorola, Inc., 644 F. Supp. 2d 788, 790-91 (N.D. Tex. 2008) (internal quotations and citations omitted); see also Broadcom Corp. v. Qualcomm Inc., 501 F.3d 297, 210 (3rd Cir. 2007) ("Industry participants who have invested significant resources developing products and technologies that conform to the standard will find it prohibitively expensive to abandon their investment and switch to another standard. They will have become 'locked in' to the standard. In this unique position of bargaining power, the patent holder may be able to extract supracompetitive royalties from the industry participants.").

[29] SEP Hearing, supra note 24, statement of Edith Ramirez, Commissioner of the FTC, at 1.

[30] Apple, Inc. v. Motorola, Inc., No. 1:11-cv-08540 (N.D. Ill.), Opinion and Order of June 22, 2012, slip op. at 18, available at http://betanews.com/wp-content/uploads/2012/06/Posner-June-22-Apple-order.pdf.

[31] SEP Hearing, supra note 24, statement of Joseph F. Wayland, at 4.

[32] FTC Report, supra note 18, at 236.

[33] Id. at 193.

[34] State Indus., Inc. v. Mor-Flo Indus., Inc., 883 F.2d 1573, 1580 (Fed. Cir. 1989).

[35] Dowagiac Mfg. Co. v. Minn. Moline Plow Co., 235 U.S. 641 (1915).

[36] Jorge L. Contreras, The February of FRAND, Mar. 6, 2012, Patently-O Patent Law Blog, at http://www.patentlyo.com/patent/2012/03/february-of-frand.html.

[37] Jorge L. Contreras, The Frand Wars: Who's on First?, April 17, 2012, Patently-O Patent Law Blog, at http://www.patentlyo.com/patent/2012/04/the-frand-wars-whos-on-first.html.

[38] Apple, Inc. v. Motorola, Inc., No. 1:11-cv-08540 (N.D. Ill.), Opinion and Order of June 22, 2012, slip op. at 18, available at http://betanews.com/wp-content/uploads/2012/06/Posner-June-22-Apple-order.pdf.

[39] Letter from Bruce Sewell, General Counsel, Apple, Inc., to Senators Leahy and Grassley, July 18, 2012,at 3, available at http://www.scribd.com/doc/100758337/Apple-to-Senate-Google-Abuses-FRAND.

[40] Colleen V. Chien, Patently Protectionist, 50 WILLIAM & MARY L. REV. 63, 70 (2008 (patent cases comprise 85% of the ITC's section 337 docket). For more information about Section 337 proceedings, see CRS Report RS22880, Intellectual Property Rights Protection and Enforcement: Section 337 of the Tariff Act of 1930, by Shayerah Ilias.

[41] 19 U.S.C. § 1337(a)(2).

[42] John Mezzalingua Assocs. v. ITC, 660 F.3d 1322, 1327-28 (Fed. Cir. 2011) (internal quotations and citation omitted).

[43] 19 U.S.C. § 1337(a)(3)(A)-(C).

[44] Omnibus Trade and Competitiveness Act of 1988, P.L. 100-418, 102 Stat. 1107 (1988).

[45] John Mezzalingua Assocs., 660 F. 3d at 1327.

[46] Russell E. Levine, The Pro's and Con's of Patent Litigation Before the International Trade Commission, at 2, available at http://apps.americanbar.org/litigation/committees/intellectual/roundtables/1106_outline.pdf.

[47] See U.S. Int'l Trade Comm'n, Section 337 Investigations: Answers to Frequently Asked Questions (March 2009), available at http://www.usitc.gov/intellectual_property/documents/337_faqs.pdf.

[48] 19 U.S.C. § 1337(j).

[49] 19 U.S.C. § 1337(j)(2).

[50] 19 U.S.C. § 1337(j)(4).

[51] 19 U.S.C. § 1337(c).

[52] 5 U.S.C. § 706(2)(E).

[53] Substantial evidence is "such relevant evidence as a reasonable mind might accept as adequate to support a conclusion." Universal Camera Corp. v. NLRB, 340 U.S. 474, 477 (1951).

[54] Cybor Corp. v. FAS Techs., Inc., 138 F.3d 1448, 1454 (Fed. Cir. 1998).

[55] Tandon Corp. v. Int'l Trade Comm'n, 831 F.2d 1017 (Fed. Cir. 1987); Texas Instr. v. Cypress, 90 F.3d 1558 (Fed. Cir. 1996).

[56] FTC Report, supra note 18, at 239.

[57] 35 U.S.C. § 283.

[58] Smith Int'l, Inc. v. Hughes Tool Co., 718 F.2d 1573, 1578 (Fed. Cir. 1983) (citation omitted).

[59] MercExchange, L.L.C. v. eBay, Inc., 401 F.3d 1323, 1338 (Fed. Cir. 2005) (citation and internal quotations omitted).

[60] eBay, Inc. v. MercExchange, L.L.C., 547 U.S. 388 (2006). For a more detailed explanation and analysis of the eBay case, see CRS Report RL33429, Availability of Injunctive Relief in Patent Cases: eBay, Inc. v. MercExchange, L.L.C., by Brian T. Yeh.

[61] eBay, 547 U.S. at 391.

[62] Id.

[63] eBay, 547 U.S. at 395 (Roberts, C.J., concurring).

[64] Id. at 396 (Kennedy, J., concurring).

[65] For more information on patent trolls, see CRS Report R42668, An Overview of the "Patent Trolls" Debate, by Brian T. Yeh.

[66] eBay, 547 U.S at 396-97.

[67] Colleen V. Chien and Mark A. Lemley, Patent Holdup, the ITC, and the Public Interest, at 9, available at https://www.law.stanford.edu/display/images/dynamic/events_media/ Panel%202%20-%20Chien%20&%20Lemley%20-%20Patent%20Holdup,%20the% 20ITC ,%20 and%20the%20Public%20Interest.pdf.

[68] Id.

[69] Id. at 11.

[70] SEP Hearing, supra note 24, statement of Edith Ramirez, at 7.

[71] Apple, Inc. v. Motorola, Inc., No. 1:11-cv-08540 (N.D. Ill.), Opinion and Order of June 22, 2012, slip op. at 18-19, available at http://betanews.com/wp-content/uploads/2012/06/Posner-June-22-Apple-order.pdf.

[72] 629 F.3d 1331 (Fed. Cir. 2010).

[73] Spansion, 629 F.3d at 1358-59 (internal citations and quotations omitted).

[74] 19 U.S.C. § 1337(d)(1).

[75] Chien and Lemley, supra note 67 at 23.

[76] Id.

[77] Id.

[78] FTC Report, supra note 18, at 240.

[79] Id.

[80] Chien and Lemley, supra note 67 at 3, 30.

[81] U.S. International Trade Commission, Facts and Trends Regarding USITC Section 337 Investigations, June 18, 2012, available at http://www.usitc.gov/press_room/ documents/featured_news/337facts.pdf.

[82] Chien and Lemley, supra note 67 at 18.

[83] P.L. 112-29, § 19 (2011).

[84] Chien and Lemley, supra note 67 at 18.

[85] See, e.g., July 9, 2012 Submission to the U.S. International Trade Commission by 19 Economics and Law Professors, Re: In the Matter of Certain Wireless Communication Devices, Portable Music and Data Processing Devices, Computers and Components

Thereof, Investigation No. 337-TA-745, at 2, available at http://digitalcommons.law.scu.edu/cgi/viewcontent.cgi?article=1436&context=facpubs.

[86] The International Trade Commission and Patent Disputes: Hearing Before the House Judiciary Committee, Subcommittee on Intellectual Property, Competition and the Internet, 112th Cong., 2d Sess., July 18, 2012 (statement of Bernard J. Cassidy, Executive Vice President & General Counsel, Tessera Technologies, Inc.), at 9 (hereinafter "ITC and Patents Hearing").

[87] U.S. Dep't of Justice, Statement of the Department of Justice's Antitrust Division on Its Decision to Close Its Investigations of Google Inc.'s Acquisition of Motorola Mobility Holdings Inc. and the Acquisitions of Certain Patents by Apple Inc., Microsoft Corp. and Research in Motion LTD., Feb. 13, 2012, available at http://www.justice.gov/atr/ public/ press_releases/2012/280190.htm.

[88] SEP Hearing, supra note 24, statement of Joseph F. Wayland, at 8.

[89] Microsoft's Support for Industry Standards, Feb. 8, 2012, available at http://www.microsoft.com/about/legal/en/us/ IntellectualProperty/iplicensing/ip2.aspx.

[90] U.S. Dep't of Justice, Statement of the Department of Justice's Antitrust Division on Its Decision to Close Its Investigations of Google Inc.'s Acquisition of Motorola Mobility Holdings Inc. and the Acquisitions of Certain Patents by Apple Inc., Microsoft Corp. and Research in Motion LTD., Feb. 13, 2012, available at http://www.justice.gov/atr/public/press_releases/2012/280190.htm.

[91] Id.

[92] Id.

[93] Id.

[94] Motorola Mobility was acquired by Google on May 22, 2012. See Press Release: Google Acquires Motorola Mobility, at http://mediacenter.motorola.com/Press-Releases/Google-Acquires-Motorola-Mobility-3aeb.aspx.

[95] John Letzing, Motorola Seeks New Licensing Deal with Microsoft, WALL ST. JOURNAL, June 21, 2012.

[96] U.S. Int'l Trade Comm'n, In the Matter of Certain Gaming and Entertainment Consoles, Related Software, and Components Thereof, Inv. No. 337-TA-752, Recommended Determination on Remedy and Bonding, May 18, 2012, available at http://www.wired.com/images_blogs/gadgetlab/2012/05/748131-480637.pdf.

[97] U.S. Int'l Trade Comm'n, In the Matter of Certain Gaming and Entertainment Consoles, Related Software, and Components Thereof, Inv. No. 337-TA-752, Notice, April 23, 2012, available at http://www.usitc.gov/press_room/ documents/337_752_ID.pdf.

[98] Members of Congress Write to ITC to Express Concern About Potential Xbox Ban, FOSS PATENTS Blog, June 12, 2012, at http://www.fosspatents.com/2012/06/members-of-congress-write-to-itc-to.html.

[99] Id.

[100] Id.

[101] Six Republican Senators Oppose Exclusion Orders Over Standard-Essential Patents, FOSS PATENTS Blog, June 28, 2012, at http://www.fosspatents.com/2012/06/six-republican-senators-oppose.html.

[102] No Xbox Import Ban in 2012: ITC Remands Investigation of Motorola Complaint, FOSS PATENTS Blog, June 29, 2012, at http://www.fosspatents.com/2012/06/no-xbox-import-ban-in-2012-itc-remands.html.

[103] Google's ITC Case Against Microsoft's Xbox to be Decided in 12 months (July 2013), FOSS PATENTS Blog, July 25, 2012, at http://www.fosspatents.com/2012/07/googles-itc-case-against-microsofts.html.

[104] In the Matter of Certain Wireless Communication Devices, Portable Music and Data Processing Devices, Computers and Components Thereof, Investigation No. 337-TA-745, Notice Regarding Initial Determination on Violation of Se4ction 337, April 24, 2012, available at http://www.usitc.gov/press_room/documents/337_745_ID.pdf.

[105] In the Matter of Certain Wireless Communication Devices, Portable Music and Data Processing Devices, Computers and Components Thereof, Investigation No. 337-TA-745, Notice of Commission Decision to Review in Part a Final Initial Determination Finding a Violation of Section 337; Request for Written Submissions, June 25, 2012, at 4-5, available at http://www.usitc.gov/secretary/fed_reg_notices/337/337_745_Notice06252012sgl.pdf.

[106] Federal Trade Commission's June 6, 2012 Submission to the U.S. International Trade Commission, Statement on the Public Interest In the Matter of Certain Wireless Communication Devices, Portable Music and Data Processing Devices, Computers and Components Thereof, Investigation No. 337-TA-745, available at http://www.ftc.gov/os/2012/ 06/1206ftcwirelesscom.pdf.

[107] July 9, 2012 Submission to the U.S. International Trade Commission by 19 Economics and Law Professors, Re: In the Matter of Certain Wireless Communication Devices, Portable Music and Data Processing Devices, Computers and Components Thereof, Investigation No. 337-TA-745, at 2, available at http://digitalcommons.law.scu.edu/cgi/ viewcontent.cgi?article=1436&context=facpubs.

[108] Id.

[109] Id.

[110] In the Matter of Certain Wireless Communication Devices, Portable Music and Data Processing Devices, Computers and Components Thereof, Investigation No. 337-TA-745, Notice of Commission Decision Finding No Violation of Section 337 as to Three Patents and Remanding the Investigation to the ALJ as to One Patent, August 24, 2012, available at http://www.usitc.gov/secretary/fed_reg_notices/337/337_745_notice08242012sgl_1.pdf.

[111] Oversight of the United States Patent and Trademark Office: Implementation of the Leahy-Smith America Invents Act and International Harmonization Efforts: Hearing Before the Senate Judiciary Committee, 112th Cong., 2d Sess., June 20, 2012, available at http://www.judiciary.senate.gov/hearings/hearing.cfm?id= d1d944e8c0b3e2a582633 afae b6ba43a.

[112] Letter from Kent Walker, General Counsel of Google, to Senators Leahy and Grassley, July 10, 2012, at 1, available at http://www.scribd.com/doc/99843544/Leahy-Grassley-Letter-Final-1-Copy.

[113] SEP Hearing, supra note 24, statement of Joseph F. Wayland, at 8.

[114] Id. at 9-10.

[115] SEP Hearing, supra note 24, statement of Edith Ramirez, at 5.

[116] Id.

[117] Id. at 6-7.

[118] Id. at 14.

[119] ITC and Patents Hearing, supra note 86, statement of Colleen V. Chien, Professor, Santa Clara University School of Law, at 1.

[120] Id. at 3.

[121] Id. at 6.

[122] July 9, 2012 Submission to the U.S. International Trade Commission by 19 Economics and Law Professors, Re: In the Matter of Certain Wireless Communication Devices, Portable Music and Data Processing Devices, Computers and Components Thereof, Investigation No. 337-TA-745, at 3, available at http://digitalcommons.l aw.scu.edu/cgi/viewcontent.cgi?article=1436&context=facpubs.

[123] ITC and Patents Hearing, supra note 86, statement of Albert Foer, president of the American Antitrust Institute, at 7.

[124] Id. at 9-10.

[125] ITC and Patents Hearing, supra note 86, statement of Bernard Cassidy, General Counsel of Tessera Technologies, Inc., at 3.

[126] Id. at 9.

[127] Id. at 10.

[128] Letter from AIPLA to the Honorable Bob Goodlatte and Mel Watt, Aug. 2, 2012, at 3-5, available at http://www.aipla.org/advocacy/congress/Documents/ AIPLA%20Letter%20to%20the%20House%20Judiciary%20Subcommittee%20on%20ITC%20and%20Patent%20Dis p utes%20-%208.2.12.pdf.

In: Standard-Essential Patent Holders
Editors: R. B. Vega and M. Guzman
ISBN: 978-1-62618-207-3

Chapter 2

STATEMENT OF SENATOR PATRICK LEAHY, CHAIRMAN, U.S. SENATE COMMITTEE ON THE JUDICIARY. HEARING ON "OVERSIGHT OF THE IMPACT ON COMPETITION OF EXCLUSION ORDERS TO ENFORCE STANDARD-ESSENTIAL PATENTS"*

In recent months, we have seen a growing number of companies engage in what some are calling the next wave in the "tech patent wars." Companies that previously cross-licensed their technologies with other companies in the market are increasingly seeking to block their competitors instead. This has the potential to harm consumers by preventing access to their favorite devices.

I have long championed the strong enforcement of our intellectual property laws because enabling inventors to profit from their work encourages innovation. Patent protection is particularly important for Vermont: the Intellectual Property Organization recently announced that in 2011 Vermont again received the most patents per capita of any state.

When inventors and developers are willing to license their technologies to one another at reasonable rates, the cross-fertilization of ideas benefits us all. But I am concerned that the recent trend of seeking exclusion orders from the International Trade Commission (ITC), rather than negotiating and seeking license fees, may have the opposite effect.

* This is an edited, reformatted and augmented version of a statement Presented July 11, 2012 before the Senate Judiciary Committee.

Today's hearing focuses on the enforcement of standard-essential patents at the ITC. Standard setting is important because it allows different companies to have their products interoperate, giving us important developments like the 3G technology used in cellular phones. To participate in the standard setting, patent owners often agree to license their patents to anyone on reasonable terms.

In March, I wrote to the administration expressing concern that ITC exclusion orders can be misused to prevent rival technologies when holders of standard-essential patents fail to reach agreement on licensing terms. These orders can pose a significant threat to competition and innovation, especially where competitors have developed products based on a mutual commitment to license standard-essential patents on reasonable terms.

Senator Lee and other Senators on this Committee have since written to the ITC expressing similar concerns. As with patent reform, this is a bipartisan issue. We have an interest on both sides of the aisle in ensuring the patent laws promote innovation and competition.

The Department of Justice and the Federal Trade Commission play a vital role in protecting consumers and competition by enforcing our nation's antitrust laws. They also have an important role in advising on antitrust issues. Congress recognized that role when it required the ITC to consult with the FTC and DOJ on competition issues that would be raised by the issuance of an exclusion order.

The testimony of today's witnesses will give the Committee a chance to further explore the competitive impact of ITC exclusion orders and whether more needs to be done to ensure consumers are not the victims of the tech patent wars.

In: Standard-Essential Patent Holders
Editors: R. B. Vega and M. Guzman
ISBN: 978-1-62618-207-3

Chapter 3

STATEMENT OF SENATOR DICK DURBIN. HEARING ON "OVERSIGHT OF THE IMPACT ON COMPETITION OF EXCLUSION ORDERS TO ENFORCE STANDARD-ESSENTIAL PATENTS"*

Mr. Chairman, thank you for holding this hearing. I appreciate the opportunity to submit a statement for the record.

In recent months a number of commenters have urged the U.S. International Trade Commission ("ITC") not to issue exclusion orders in cases where standard essential patents ("SEPs") have been found to be infringed.

To justify their position, these commenters have typically cited concerns about the possibility of "patent hold-up" by holders of SEPs.While there is indeed always a possibility that such patent hold-up might occur, any calls to limit the availability of ITC exclusion orders for SEPs or to limit the use of the ITC as a forum for disputes involving imported products that allegedly infringe on SEPs should be made based on *actual data* that demonstrates that our current system has a problem – and not on the mere possibility of a problem.

There is legitimate concern that any changes made to our current system in the absence of such data could unduly favor infringers and prove detrimental to innovators, consumers, and competition at large.

* This is an edited, reformatted and augmented version of a statement Presented July 11, 2012 before the Senate Judiciary Committee.

Our current system of patent protection, with ITC playing its key enforcement role, has a long history of working well to encourage innovation and stimulate competition. When complaints of unfair practices arise, case-by-case adjudication of such complaints, including adjudication by the ITC, has been effective in striking the right balance between the interests of patentholders, alleged infringers and the public. Any significant changes to the current system should be cautiously considered in order to ensure that this balance is not unsettled.

The complexities involved in maintaining this balance are evident when it comes to SEPs. When a company agrees to contribute its patented technology to an industry standard, the company commits to negotiate to license the patent on fair, reasonable and nondiscriminatory (F/RAND) terms. While in those negotiations there is always a possibility that a company that has made a F/RAND commitment will seek to use the availability of an exclusion order as leverage to try to obtain better licensing terms, there is an equivalent concern that without the availability of an exclusion order a company using a SEP will hold out for less-than-reasonable licensing terms or will simply infringe on the patent and engage in protracted infringement litigation in court while avoiding paying royalties until the litigation is over. In fast-moving sectors such as the consumer technology sector, such potentially bad-faith behavior by user companies could significantly harm patentholding companies or could incent patentholders not to participate in standard setting processes in the future. Competition and consumers could be detrimentally impacted as a result. For reasons such as these, we should tread carefully when considering changes to the current system of SEP enforcement.

As this Committee proceeds with its consideration of this issue, I hope we will ask for and obtain hard data from our witnesses and from other stakeholders. I also hope we will solicit the views of stakeholders who are not represented at the witness table today, such as the ITC, the Patent and Trademark Office, the U.S. Trade Representative, small technology companies, standard-setting organizations, and consumer groups. Such data and views will help inform our analysis as we consider potential changes to the current patent protection system.

In: Standard-Essential Patent Holders
Editors: R. B. Vega and M. Guzman
ISBN: 978-1-62618-207-3

Chapter 4

STATEMENT OF JOSEPH F. WAYLAND, ACTING ASSISTANT ATTORNEY GENERAL, ANTITRUST DIVISION, U.S. DEPARTMENT OF JUSTICE. HEARING ON "OVERSIGHT OF THE IMPACT ON COMPETITION OF EXCLUSION ORDERS TO ENFORCE STANDARD-ESSENTIAL PATENTS"*

INTRODUCTION

Good morning, Mr. Chairman and Ranking Member. It is a pleasure to have this opportunity to discuss the Antitrust Division's experience with standard-essential patents. I joined the Division in September 2010, as Deputy Assistant Attorney General for Civil Enforcement. At the end of April, I assumed the role of Acting Assistant Attorney General (AAG). Both former AAG Christine Varney and former Acting AAG Sharis Pozen provided strong leadership and vision for the Division's mission to protect and promote competition, and I hope to follow their lead.

The issues I will discuss today involve three important inputs to our modern innovation-based economy: patent rights, competition, and collaboratively set standards. These inputs drive innovation in complementary,

* This is an edited, reformatted and augmented version of a statement presented July 11, 2012 before the Senate Judiciary Committee.

though different ways. In our system, antitrust and intellectual property policy function together to provide consumers with high-quality products and services at competitive prices, while at the same time preserving strong incentives for the innovation that creates and improves those products.

Innovation is the key to economic growth in the United States. It creates new products and new jobs, and maintains our competitiveness in the global economy. As the Commerce Department reported in 2010, it is the introduction of new products and processes for making those products that has been responsible for three-quarters of the growth in the U.S. economy since World War II. Arti Rai et al., Patent Reform: Unleashing Innovation, Promoting Economic Growth & Producing High-Paying Jobs 2 (U.S. Dep't of Commerce, Apr. 13, 2010).

Patents have long played a central role in promoting innovation and economic growth by encouraging individuals and companies to apply their knowledge, take risks, and make investments in research and development. These efforts, in turn, have benefitted society as a whole by providing new and valuable technologies, lower prices, improved quality, and increased consumer choice. *See, e.g.*, *2010 Joint Strategic Plan on Intellectual Property Enforcement* 5 (June 2010), *available at* www.whitehouse. gov/sites/default/files/omb/assets/intellectualproperty/intellectual_property_strategic_plan.pdf.

Competition also creates incentives for invention, innovation, and risk-taking by allowing competitors to profit from being at the forefront of technological change. The desire to improve existing products to maintain or gain market share pushes competitors to improve function, design, and production processes, while visionaries leap beyond existing know-how to introduce radically new products and services that transform the lives of consumers—inventions ranging from DNA testing and sequencing and microprocessors to anti-retroviral treatments, file compression, digital content streaming, and cloud computing.

Standards also drive our economy. Standards have a range of benefits, from helping to protect public health and safety to promoting efficient resource allocation and production by allowing for interoperability among complementary products. Standards are not new: For example, the adoption of standard gauge rails in 1866 eliminated network incompatibilities between the seven different types of rail gauge then in use and supported our nation's westward expansion. Today, standards underpin efforts to drive and deploy electronic vehicles, share and protect health information, and enable the use of smart grids for the delivery of electricity. Interoperability standards have also paved the way for the complex communications networks and sophisticated mobile computing devices that have become hallmarks of the modern age.

Standard-Setting and Competition

The Antitrust Division has worked closely with our sister antitrust agency, the Federal Trade Commission (FTC), and with other federal agencies, including the U.S. Patent and Trademark Office, an agency of the Department of Commerce, to better understand the interface between standards and antitrust and to promote intellectual property practices for standard-setting activities that preserve competition and protect consumers. For example, in 2007, the Antitrust Division and the FTC issued a joint report on the intersection of intellectual property rights and competition that addresses a number of critical standard-setting issues. In particular, the agencies found that when a standard incorporates patented technology owned by a participant in the standard-setting process and that standard becomes established, switching in some cases becomes difficult and expensive, and that the particular technology may gain market power. *See* U.S. DEP'T OF JUSTICE & FED. TRADE COMM'N, ANTITRUST ENFORCEMENT AND INTELLECTUAL PROPERTY RIGHTS: PROMOTING INNOVATION AND COMPETITION 35-36 (2007). This creates the potential for patent holders to take advantage of that market power by engaging in one form of what is known as patent hold-up, such as by excluding a competitor from a market or obtaining an unjustifiably higher price for its invention than would have been possible before the standard was set. This raises particular concerns when alternative technologies could have been included in the standard. Patent hold-up can cause other problems as well. For example, it may induce users to postpone or avoid incorporating standardized technology in their products. Consumers of the products using the standard could also be harmed to the extent that companies implementing the standard pass on higher royalties in the form of a higher price.

To reduce the occurrences of this type of opportunistic conduct, standard-setting organizations (SSOs) commonly include in their patent policies commitments from participants to license the patents they own that are essential to the standard (standard-essential patents) on "reasonable and non-discriminatory" (RAND) or "fair, reasonable, and non-discriminatory" (FRAND) terms. Participation in relevant standards bodies is voluntary, but in some cases the licensing commitment is a condition of participation in the standards body, or the license commitment may be voluntary or offer a mechanism for opting out of the obligation to license essential patents. (In the United States, SSO members commit to license all of their standards-essential patents on RAND terms, while in other jurisdictions SSO members commit to license such patents on FRAND terms. We use F/RAND to refer to both types of commitments as they are substantively the same type of commitment.) SSOs and their members rely on F/RAND commitments to facilitate the bilateral licensing of patents that are needed to allow a standard to become successful and to provide assurances to implementers of the standard that the patented technologies will be available to those willing and able to license them. By participating in the standard-setting activities and making a F/RAND licensing commitment, some have argued that the patent holder foregoes its right to exclude where the standard is being implemented. In making the voluntary licensing commitment, a patent holder that also sells products and services related to the standard benefits from expanded marketing opportunities, and patent holders that focus on licensing their inventions benefit from an expanded source of revenue.

The Antitrust Division has stressed that SSOs that set forth well-defined patent policy rules that minimize ambiguity can effectively promote competition. My predecessor, Christine Varney, explained that "[e]ven without saying what rules are best, it is at least plain that clearer rules will allow for more informed participation and will enable participants to make more knowledgeable decisions regarding implementation of the standard. Clarity alone does not eliminate the possibility of hold-up ... but it is a step in the right direction." Christine Varney, Assistant Attorney Gen., Antitrust Div., U.S. Dep't of Justice, Remarks as Prepared for the Joint Workshop of the U.S. Patent and Trademark Office, the Federal Trade Commission, and the Department of Justice on the Intersection of Patent Policy and Competition Policy: Implications for Promoting Innovation 8 (May 26, 2010).

For example, in 2006 and 2007, we advised IEEE and VITA that requiring or permitting patent holders participating in a standard-setting process to disclose the most restrictive terms on which they were willing to license their essential patents—that is, patents that were declared essential to the standard for uses implementing the standard— could preserve competition and avoid unreasonable licensing terms that might harm the successful adoption and implementation of the standard. Letter from Thomas O. Barnett, Assistant Attorney Gen., U.S. Dep't of Justice, to Michael A. Lindsey, Esq. (April 30, 2007), *available at* www.justice.gov/atr/public/busreview/222978.pdf (IEEE Business Review); Letter from Thomas O. Barnett, Assistant Attorney Gen.,

U.S. Dep't of Justice, to Robert A. Skitol, Esq. (Oct. 30, 2006), available at www.justice.gov/atr/public/usreview/219380.pdf (VITA Business Review). IEEE and VITA incorporated this element into their patent policies by creating options that seek to limit some of the ambiguity associated with commitments to license on F/RAND terms. I encourage other SSOs that want to revise their patent policies to seek ex ante review of them through our business review procedures if the proposed revisions could impact competition.

The Antitrust Division's Investigations Involving Standard-Setting Activities

In addition to encouraging standard setting practices that benefit competition and consumers, the Antitrust Division has also pursued enforcement where appropriate. Notably, the Antitrust Division has conducted a number of investigations involving standard-essential patents involving mobile devices. The mobile-device industry is in technological transition, where smartphones are replacing previously dominant feature cell phones at lightning speed and new computer products, such as computer tablets, have been introduced into the market. Smartphones combine the best features of cell phones with the features of computers that are most useful to mobile users, such as access to the Internet and email functionality. As a result, new technological innovators have displaced some established manufacturers of feature phones, and large portfolios of patents have been offered for sale. The Division had concerns about the F/RANDencumbered standard-essential patents because wireless devices, including smartphones and tablets, typically implement a significant number of telecommunication and computer standards—including cellular air interface, wireless broadband, and video compression standards.

In February 2012, the Antitrust Division closed its investigations of the acquisition of two significant patent portfolios. The first involved Rockstar Bidco (a partnership that included Apple, Microsoft, Research in Motion, Sony, and Ericsson) and its acquisition of 6,000 patents and patent applications from Nortel at a bankruptcy auction. The Nortel portfolio also included a number of patents that Nortel had committed to license on F/RAND terms for uses associated with certain standards, including wireless standards. The second involved Google's acquisition of Motorola Mobility, a manufacturer of smartphones and tablet computers and the holder of 17,000 issued patents and 6,800 patent applications. Motorola had made commitments to several SSOs to license hundreds of these patents on F/RAND terms for uses related to the standards, which included both cellular air interface and Wi-Fi standards.

In both matters, the Division's investigations focused on whether the acquiring firms would have the incentive and ability to exploit ambiguities in the commitments the sellers made to license their patents on F/RAND terms to hold up implementers of the standard in a manner that would raise rivals' costs or foreclose competition, to the detriment of consumers. For example, the acquiring firms might seek to raise rivals' costs by demanding higher licensing rates, compelling cross licenses to differentiating IP valued in excess of the F/RAND rate, charging licensees the entire portfolio royalty rate when licensing only a small subset of the patents in its portfolio, or seeking to prevent or exclude products that infringed these patents from the market altogether. We investigated whether the patent acquisitions would change the incentives or abilities of the new owners to obtain higher royalties from their competitors, particularly by using the threat of an injunction or exclusion order.

After thorough investigations in both matters, the Division concluded that neither acquisition was likely to substantially lessen competition for wireless devices. In particular, we determined that neither Research in Motion nor Microsoft was likely to use any standard-essential F/RAND-encumbered patents from the Nortel portfolio to harm their rivals by excluding them from the markets or charging supracompetitive royalties, because they would be unable to attract a sufficient number of customers to purchase their smartphones to make up for the loss of licensing revenue. In addition, we found that Microsoft previously entered cross-license agreements with the majority of its Android-based OEM competitors and that its newly acquired patents would be included in these agreements.

With respect to Google, there was evidence that Motorola Mobility had a long history of licensing its F/RAND-encumbered standard-essential patents and had been engaged in extended disputes with Apple, Microsoft, and others before Google sought to acquire the company and its patent portfolio. We did not believe that transferring ownership of the patents from Motorola to Google would substantially change that practice. Moreover, while we were investigating these transactions, Apple stated in a letter to the European Telecommunications Standards Institute (ETSI), the body that develops many wireless standards in Europe, that the company would not use F/RAND-encumbered standard-essential patents to exclude rivals from the wireless market by seeking injunctions for infringement. Similarly, Microsoft posted a public statement on its website explaining that it would not seek injunctions or exclusion orders based on F/RAND-encumbered standard-essential patents. Google also publicly revealed its licensing policy, stating that it would not seek injunctive relief in disputes involving future license revenues provided that the potential licensee (a) forgoes certain defenses such as challenging the validity of the patent; (b) pays the full disputed licensing amount into escrow; and (c) agrees to a reciprocal process regarding injunctions. The commitments made by Apple and Microsoft substantially lessened the Antitrust Division's concerns about potential anticompetitive use of F/RAND-encumbered standard-essential patents. The Antitrust Division observed that Google's commitments did not provide the same direct confirmation of its F/RAND-encumbered standard-essential patent licensing policies.

Although we concluded that the acquisitions of these patent portfolios were not likely to substantially lessen competition, the Antitrust Division noted its concerns about the potential inappropriate use of F/RAND-encumbered standard-essential patents to disrupt competition and specifically limited our conclusion to the transfer of ownership rights and not to the exercise of those transferred rights. We have continued closely to monitor the use of F/RAND-encumbered standard-essential patents in the wireless device industry, particularly as they relate to smartphones and computer tablets, to ensure that they do not stifle competition and innovation in this important industry.

The Antitrust Division is also closely monitoring a number of pending International Trade Commission (ITC) matters involving F/RAND-encumbered SEPs. *See 19 U.S.C. §1337(b)* (directing the Commission to consult with the Department of Justice). In determining whether to issue exclusion orders, the ITC is directed to consider the "effect of exclusion upon the public health and welfare, competitive conditions in the United States economy, the production of like or directly competitive articles in the United States, and United States consumers." *Id.* As the ITC has observed, these public interest factors "are not meant to be given mere lip service," but rather "public health and welfare and the assurance of competitive conditions in the United States economy must be the *overriding considerations* in the administration of this statute." *Certain Inclined Field Acceleration Tubes and Components Thereof*, Inv. No. 337-TA-67, USITC Pub. 1119, Comm'n Op., at 22 (Dec. 1980), *quoting* S. REP. 93-1298, at 197 (1974), *reprinted in* 1974 U.S.C.C.A.N. 7186, 7330. For example, the ITC could determine that an exclusion order is not in the public interest even where infringement is found because the value or importance of the infringed patent to the assembled good is dwarfed by the overall value of the assembled good or the patented aspect is not important to the operation of the good, and a broad exclusion order would be tantamount to denying the public the assembled good for a period of time.

In seeking public comment, the Department of Justice believes the ITC should continue to gather the types of information necessary to evaluate whether the statutory public interest factors counsel against the imposition of an exclusion order. In considering this issue, the Department of Justice is concerned about the circumstances in which an exclusion order may be inappropriate, in certain cases where a product implementing a standard has been determined to have infringed a valid F/RANDencumbered patent that is essential to that standard. Federal courts have begun to consider the appropriateness of injunctive relief based on factors laid out in the Supreme Court's eBay decision and similar considerations could arise in ITC public interest determinations. Certain conduct outside of the standard setting context could similarly give rise to questions about the appropriateness of an exclusion order. In an era where competition thrives on interconnected, interoperable network platforms, these considerations merit special attention. For example, if the ITC concludes exclusion orders may be inappropriate in the scenarios described above, it may be appropriate for it to determine whether it has the authority to stay the imposition of an exclusion order contingent on the infringing party's commitment to abide by an arbitrator's determination of the fair value of a license.

This concludes my prepared remarks. I would be happy to answer any further questions the Committee may have.

In: Standard-Essential Patent Holders
Editors: R. B. Vega and M. Guzman
ISBN: 978-1-62618-207-3

Chapter 5

STATEMENT OF EDITH RAMIREZ, COMISSIONER, FEDERAL TRADE COMMISSION. HEARING ON "OVERSIGHT OF THE IMPACT ON COMPETITION OF EXCLUSION ORDERS TO ENFORCE STANDARD-ESSENTIAL PATENTS"*

Chairman Leahy, Ranking Member Grassley, and Members of the Committee, thank you for the opportunity to appear before you today. I am Edith Ramirez, Commissioner of the Federal Trade Commission (FTC), and I am pleased to testify on behalf of the FTC to discuss the impact on competition of injunctive relief, including an International Trade Commission (ITC) exclusion order, to enforce standard-essential patents.[1] The testimony focuses on standard-essential patents (SEPs) that a patent holder has committed to license on reasonable and nondiscriminatory (RAND) terms.[2] Simply put, the FTC is concerned that a patent holder may use the threat of an ITC exclusion order, or an injunction issued in district court, to "hold-up" or demand higher royalties or other more costly licensing terms after the standard is implemented than could have been obtained before its IP was included in the standard. Federal district courts have the tools to address this issue, by balancing equitable factors or awarding money damages,[3] and the FTC believes that the ITC likewise has the authority under its public interest

* This is an edited, reformatted and augmented version of a statement Presented July 11, 2012 before the Senate Judiciary Committee.

obligations to address this concern and limit the potential for hold-up.[4] If the ITC finds that its public interest authority is not flexible enough to prevent hold-up, then Congress should consider whether legislative remedies are necessary.

To explain the Commission's position, this statement (1) outlines the common ground between intellectual property and competition law and the Commission's prior policy work in the IP arena; (2) describes the FTC's definition of hold-up in the standard setting context; (3)explains the potential for divergent outcomes in federal district court and ITC litigation; and (4) highlights concerns that the FTC recently presented to the ITC on this issue.

I. Intellectual Property and Competition Laws Work Together to Promote Innovation

Intellectual property and competition laws share the fundamental goals of promoting innovation and consumer welfare. Patents encourage investments in innovation by enabling the patent holder to prevent others from appropriating the value of its technology without compensation. Because the patent system requires public disclosure, it also promotes the distribution of scientific and technical information that would not otherwise occur. Competition stimulates innovation by creating an incentive for the pursuit of new or better products or processes. Companies may compete to be the first to market with a new technology, or they may invent new, lower-cost, ways to meet existing needs. Competition drives such innovation most effectively if patent law protects the innovator from those that would copy its innovation. Patent law serves its intended purpose if it protects such innovation and does not inadvertently serve as a barrier to it. Modern understanding of these two bodies of law recognizes that intellectual property and competition law can work together to bring new and better products, technologies, and services to consumers more efficiently and at lower prices.

For almost two decades, the Federal Trade Commission has recognized the tandem role of intellectual property and competition in its policy and enforcement efforts. For example, in 1995, the Commission and the Department of Justice issued enforcement guidelines that recognize that licensing intellectual property can facilitate integration of the licensed property with complementary factors of production, which can benefit consumers through the reduction of costs and the introduction of new products.[5] In 2003, the Commission issued its first major report on the patent system, focusing on the impact of patent quality on innovation and competition.[6] In 2007, the Commission and the Department of Justice jointly issued a report emphasizing the need to account properly for the pro-competitive benefits of patent rights in antitrust analysis and enforcement policy.[7] The 2007 Report addresses the potential for hold-up after technology has been chosen by an SSO, and discusses ways that SSOs can adopt policies to avoid or deter this result.[8] In our latest study in March 2011, *The Evolving IP Marketplace: Aligning Patent Notice and Remedies with Competition*,[9] the Commission considered how patent notice and remedies affect innovation, competition, and consumer welfare. In particular, we recommended a number of reforms to the laws associated with patent notice and remedies to limit the risks to innovation and competition that arise when patents are asserted after substantial investments are made to bring a product to market. We also recommended mechanisms that district courts and the ITC can use to mitigate hold-up when resolving disputes involving SEPs.[10] The 2011 report was based, in part, on a joint hearing co-sponsored by the Commission, the DOJ, and the Patent and Trademark Office.

The FTC's recent statement to the ITC builds on our earlier policy and enforcement efforts, in particular our competitive concerns with companies seeking injunctive relief for RAND-encumbered SEPs, and highlights the critical role that intellectual property and competition play in promoting innovation.

II. Standard Setting Organizations and the Potential for Hold-Up

Firms in the information technology and telecommunications industries frequently face the problem that hundreds, thousands, and sometimes hundreds of thousands of different claimed inventions need to work together in a single device and in multiple devices operating together within a system. They solve this "interoperability" problem through voluntary consensus standard setting conducted by SSOs. SSOs create standards that ensure that devices within a system will work together and communicate with each other in standardized, predictable ways. Such standards can create enormous value for consumers by increasing competition, innovation, product quality, and choice. However, incorporating patented technologies into standards also has the potential to distort competition by enabling SEP owners to use the leverage they acquire as a result of the standard setting process to negotiate high royalty rates and other favorable terms after a standard is adopted that they could not have credibly demanded beforehand.

The possibility of patent hold-up derives from changes in the relative costs of technologies as a result of the standard setting process.[11] Prior to adoption of a standard, alternative technologies compete to be included in the standard, on the basis of features, quality, or price. Often there are a number of technologies, with similar attributes, available for inclusion in the standard; and while it may be possible for SSO members to negotiate licenses for SEPs before a standard is adopted, this is not a realistic option for many firms that may implement the standard. Instead, more often SSO members delay this decision and require that the owner of the technology agree to license SEPs on RAND terms as a *quid pro quo* for the inclusion of their patents in a standard. This makes it easier to adopt a standard, but also creates the potential for hold-up because it defers the negotiation on price until after the standard is adopted. Once a standard is adopted, an entire industry begins to make investments tied to the standard. Because it may not be feasible to deviate from the standard unless all or most other participants in the industry agree to do so in compatible ways, and because all of these participants may face substantial switching costs in abandoning initial designs and substituting a different technology, an entire industry may become locked in to a standard. This gives a SEP owner the ability to demand and obtain royalty payments much higher than might have been available prior to adoption of the standard because these rates need not be based on the true market value of its patents, but instead on the costs and delays of switching away from the standardized technology. In other words, as Judge Posner noted, "once a patent becomes essential to a standard, the patentee's bargaining power surges because a prospective licensee has no alternative to licensing the patent; he is at the patentee's mercy."[12] This is one form of "hold-up."

Hold-up and the threat of hold-up can deter innovation by increasing costs and uncertainty for other industry participants, including other patent holders.[13] The threat of holdup also may reduce the value of standard setting, leading firms to rely less on the standard setting process and depriving consumers of the substantial pro-competitive benefits of standardized technology.

RAND commitments are designed to mitigate the risk of patent hold-up, and encourage investment in the standard.[14] After a RAND commitment is made, the patent holder and the company that wants to implement the technology will typically negotiate a royalty or, in the event they are unable to agree, may seek judicial determination of a reasonable rate. A patent holder may also seek an injunction from a district court, or an exclusion order from the ITC. A royalty negotiation that occurs under threat of an injunction or an exclusion order may be weighted heavily in favor of the patent holder in a way that is in tension with the RAND commitment. High switching costs combined with the threat of an exclusion order could allow a patent holder to obtain unreasonable licensing terms despite its RAND commitment, whether or not the invention is highly valuable on its own, because implementers are locked into practicing the standard. This is an even bigger problem when the hold-up creates a very high cost for a very small component of the overall product. In these ways, the threat of injunctive relief, including an exclusion order, may allow the holder of a RAND-encumbered SEP to realize royalty rates that reflect patent hold-up, rather than the value of the patent relative to alternatives.[15] This can raise prices to consumers, distort incentives to innovate, and undermine the standard setting process.

III. Differences Between Injunction Analysis in Federal District Court and Exclusion Orders in the ITC

Until 2006, permanent injunctive relief was virtually automatic following a district court's finding of infringement. Courts followed a general rule, established by the Federal Circuit, in favor of granting injunctions based on a presumption of irreparable harm.[16] In a 2006 decision, *eBay v. MercExchange, L.L.C.*, a unanimous Supreme Court rejected the presumption of irreparable harm and other categorical approaches in favor of a case-by-case application of "traditional equitable principles,"[17] including requiring proof of the patent holder's irreparable harm and the inadequacy of money damages. Under *eBay*'s equitable analysis, it may be difficult for RAND-encumbered SEP holders to show that money damages are inadequate because they have already committed to license their intellectual property on RAND terms.

In a recent decision, Judge Posner, sitting by designation in the Northern District of Illinois, applied *eBay*'s equitable analysis to find that a patent holder would not be entitled to an injunction for infringement of a FRAND-encumbered SEP. "I don't see how, given FRAND, I would be justified in enjoining [the alleged infringer] from infringing the [patent-in-suit] unless

Apple refuses to pay a royalty that meets the FRAND requirement."[18] He continued, "[b]y committing to license its patents on FRAND terms, [the patent holder] committed to license the [patent--in-suit] to anyone willing to pay a FRAND royalty and thus implicitly acknowledged that a royalty is adequate compensation for a license to use that patent."[19] The patent holder, therefore, could not satisfy *eBay*'s requirement that money damages would provide inadequate relief.[20] Because a FRAND royalty would adequately compensate a patent holder, Judge Posner determined that an injunction was not warranted in that case.[21]

Although all federal district courts must follow the equitable *eBay* injunction analysis, the ITC, another venue in which patentees may litigate, does not.[22] That discrepancy has generated concern that the ITC now is attracting litigation by patent holders that are less likely to meet the requirements to obtain an injunction in federal court, potentially leading to hold-up and any related consumer harm.[23]

The ITC is a quasi-judicial, independent federal agency established by Congress with a wide range of trade-related mandates, among them intellectual property-based import investigations. Patent holders that believe imported products infringe their patents may file a complaint with the ITC under Section 337 of the Tariff Act of 1930. The statute prohibits unfair methods of competition, including patent infringement, from goods imported into the United States.[24] The ITC has *in rem* jurisdiction over the imported goods, which allows patent holders to bring cases against foreign defendants that might otherwise be outside the jurisdiction of U.S. district courts. After finding patent infringement, the ITC may issue a cease and desist order and an exclusion order. A cease and desist order prohibits a defendant from selling infringing imported articles out of U.S. inventory.[25] An exclusion order directs the U.S. Customs Service to bar infringing articles from entry into the United States.[26] ITC cease and desist and exclusion orders are subject to review by the President, or his designee the United States Trade Representative, and appealable to the Federal Circuit. The ITC cannot award monetary damages for past infringement.

Section 337 provides a mechanism by which the ITC can limit the incidence of hold-up generated by an exclusion order and the harm to consumers that may result from such orders. It allows the ITC to consider "the public health and welfare, competitive conditions in the United States economy, the production of like or directly competitive articles in the United States, and United States consumers" in deciding whether to grant an exclusion order.[27] However, the ITC has rarely used this provision to deny an exclusion order.[28] Assertion of a patent against a standard in the presence of a RAND commitment, however, creates a particularly important scenario for considering the public interest, and Section 337's language should allow consideration of how an exclusion order can cause hold-up, distort "competitive conditions" by forcing negotiation under the shadow of switching costs, impair innovation, and harm "United States consumers." By incorporating these economic concepts into its remedy analysis, the ITC would move that analysis closer to that required in district courts by *eBay* and promote the beneficial and efficient operation of intellectual property and competition law.[29]

IV. Potential Harm to Competition Arising from Exclusion Orders for Infringement of a RAND-Encumbered SEP

Consistent with the requirement of Congress that the FTC and ITC consult in 337 investigations,[30] on June 6, 2012, the FTC responded to the ITC's request for statements on the public interest in two Section 337 investigations.[31] The FTC explained the potential economic and competitive impact of injunctive relief for infringement of RAND-encumbered SEPs. Although the FTC rarely weighs in on ITC proceedings, it filed this statement because these investigations appear to present an issue of first impression for the ITC: the competitive implications of granting an exclusion order for infringement of a SEP that the patent holder has committed to license on RAND terms.[32]

The FTC agrees that an appropriately granted exclusion order preserves the exclusivity that forms the foundation of the patent system's incentives to innovate, and the threat of an exclusion order can provide a significant deterrent to infringement.[33] RAND-encumbered SEPs, which include commitments to license, require additional considerations before evaluating whether the exclusion order is appropriate because they present considerably different issues than patents that are not encumbered by a commitment to license. A RAND commitment provides evidence that the SEP owner planned to monetize its IP through broad licensing on reasonable terms rather than through exclusive use – and thus would not likely be irreparably harmed by money damages.[34] Consistent with the proper role of the patent system, remedies that reduce the chance of patent hold-up can encourage innovation by increasing certainty for firms investing in standards-compliant products and complementary technologies. Reducing hold-up also better aligns the reward from innovation with its true value to consumers. Remedies that reduce hold-up improve the working of the standard setting system and prevent the price increases associated with patent hold-up without reducing incentives to innovate.

ITC issuance of an exclusion or cease and desist order in matters involving RAND-encumbered SEPs, where infringement is based on implementation of standardized technology, has the potential to cause substantial harm to U.S. competition, consumers and innovation. The FTC expressed concern to the ITC that a patent holder can make a RAND commitment as part of the standard setting process, and then seek an exclusion order for infringement of the RAND-encumbered SEP as a way of securing royalties that may be inconsistent with that RAND commitment.

The ITC has a statutory obligation to consider "competitive conditions in the United States economy ... and United States consumers[,]"[35] and to refrain from imposing Section 337 remedies in conflict with the public interest. The FTC proposed a range of remedies that would be consistent with this obligation. For example, the ITC could find that Section 337's public interest factors support denial of an exclusion order if the holder of the RAND-encumbered SEP has not complied with its RAND obligation, which would include a duty to negotiate with potential licensees in good faith.[36] In the Initial Determination of Investigation No. 337-TA-752, the ITC administrative law judge found that, "the royalty rate of Motorola of 2.25%, both as to its amount and the products covered, could not possibly have been accepted by Microsoft."[37] While this approach may leave the patent holder without a remedy in the ITC, a remedy in district court would remain available. Alternatively, the ITC could delay the effective date of its Section 337 remedies until the parties mediate in good faith for damages for past infringement and/or an ongoing royalty for future licensed use, with the parties facing the respective risks that the exclusion order will (i) eventually go into effect if the implementer refuses a reasonable offer or (ii) be vacated if the ITC finds that the patent holder has refused to accept a reasonable offer.[38] The FTC urged the ITC to follow the requirements of Sections 337(d)(1) and (f)(1) and consider the impact of patent hold-up on competitive conditions and United States consumers in cases that address RAND-encumbered SEPs.

After the FTC filed its statement, the ITC indicated that it is particularly interested in the public interest issues concerning RAND commitments and exclusion orders. In late June, the ITC issued a Notice of Review in one of its investigations.[39] The Notice seeks briefing from the parties on eight RAND-related topics, including whether: (1) "the mere existence of a RAND obligation preclude[s] issuance of an exclusion order[;]" (2) a patent owner that has refused to offer or negotiate a license on RAND terms should be able to obtain an exclusion order; and (3) a patent owner should be able to obtain an exclusion order if it has offered a RAND license, and that license has been rejected by the alleged infringer.[40]

The FTC believes that the ITC has the authority under its public interest obligations to resolve all of these questions, and to deny an exclusion order if the holder of the RAND-encumbered SEP has not complied with its RAND obligation. If, instead, the ITC finds that its public interest authority is not flexible enough to allow this analysis, then Congress should consider whether it should amend Section 337 to give the ITC more flexible authority to prevent hold-up.

Thank you for this opportunity to share the Commission's views. We look forward to working with you on this important issue.

End Notes

[1] The written statement represents the views of the Federal Trade Commission. My oral presentation and responses to questions are my own and do not necessarily reflect the views of the Commission or of any other Commissioner.
Commissioner Rosch concurs in the submission of this testimony, but, as he has previously stated (see infra note 3), he is of the view that the issuance of injunctive relief, including an ITC exclusion order, is inappropriate where the patent holder has made a RAND commitment for a standard essential patent, even if the patentee has met its RAND obligation. In his view, a RAND pledge appears to be, by its very nature, a commitment to license; if so, seeking injunctive relief would be inconsistent with that commitment. Commissioner Rosch thus submits that if a court concludes that a party, or its predecessor in interest, made a RAND commitment with respect to a SEP, an injunction should be denied for that patent. He finds instructive the Supreme Court's eBay decision, which held that injunctive relief should be granted only when "monetary damages . . . are inadequate to compensate for [the] injury." eBay v. MercExchange, L.L.C., 547 U.S. 388, 391 (2006). He also believes that injunctive relief is arguably contrary to the public interest when a cross-license covered by non-SEP patents is sought because injunctive relief would seem to deter innovation in those circumstances.

[2] The Testimony uses the term RAND, but the analysis applies equally to intellectual property that a patent holder has committed to license on fair, reasonable and non-discriminatory (FRAND) terms.

[3] See, e.g., Apple, Inc. v. Motorola, Inc., 2012 WL 2376664, at *12-13 (N.D. Ill. June 22, 2012) (Judge Posner, sitting by designation in the Northern District of Illinois, denied injunctive

relief, in part, because a RAND royalty would provide all necessary relief to the holder of a standard-essential patent committed to RAND terms).

[4] See Third Party United States Federal Trade Commission's Statement on the Public Interest filed on June 6, 2012 in In re Certain Wireless Communication Devices, Portable Music & Data Processing Devices, Computers and Components Thereof, Inv. No. 337-TA-745, available at www.ftc.gov/os/2012/06/1206ftcwirelesscom.pdf and in In re Certain Gaming and Entertainment Consoles, Related Software, and Components Thereof, Inv. No. 337-TA-752, available at http://www.ftc.gov/os/2012/06/1206ftcgamingconsole.pdf.

[5] See U.S. Dep't of Justice & Fed. Trade Comm'n, Antitrust Guidelines for the Licensing of Intellectual Property (1995), available at http://www.ftc.gov/bc/0558.pdf.

[6] Fed. Trade Comm'n, To Promote Innovation: The Proper Balance of Competition and Patent Law and Policy (2003) ("2003 Report"), available at http://www.ftc.gov/os/2003/10/ innovationrpt.pdf. Justice Kennedy cited the 2003 Report in his concurrence in eBay v. MercExchange, L.L.C., 547 U.S. 388, 396 (2006).

[7] See U.S. Dep't of Justice & Fed. Trade Comm'n, Antitrust Enforcement and Intellectual Property Rights Promoting Innovation and Competition 46-47 ("2007 Report"), available at http://www.ftc.gov/reports/innovation/P040101PromotingInnovationandCompetitionrpt0704.pdf.

[8] 2007 Report, Ch. 2.

[9] Fed. Trade Comm'n, The Evolving IP Marketplace: Aligning Patent Notice and Remedies with Competition ("2011 Report"), available at http://www.ftc.gov/os/2011/03/ 110307 patentreport.pdf.

[10] 2011 Report at 191-93 and 239-44.

[11] Joseph Farrell et al., Standard Setting, Patents and Hold-Up, 74 ANTITRUST L.J. 603, 607-08 (2007).

[12] Apple, Inc. v. Motorola, Inc., 2012 WL 2376664, at *11 (N.D. Ill. June 22, 2012).

[13] See generally 2011 Report and 2007 Report.

[14] 2007 Report at 46-47.

[15] See Apple, Inc., 2012 WL 2376664, at *12 (quoting the FTC's explanation of the potential economic and competitive impact of injunctive relief on disputes involving SEPs).

[16] Richardson v. Suzuki Motor Co., 868 F.2d 1226, 1246-47 (Fed. Cir. 1989) (citations omitted).

[17] eBay v. MercExchange, L.L.C., 547 U.S. 388, 391 (2006). The Court listed four factors that a patent holder must satisfy to obtain an injunction: "A plaintiff must demonstrate: (1) that it has suffered an irreparable injury; (2) that remedies available at law, such as monetary damages, are inadequate to compensate for that injury; (3) that, considering the balance of hardships between the plaintiff and defendant, a remedy in equity is warranted; and (4) that the public interest would not be disserved by a permanent injunction." Id.

[18] Apple, Inc., 2012 WL 2376664, at *12; see also eBay, 547 U.S. at 400 (Kennedy, J., concurring) (noting that hold-up results when "an injunction, and the potentially serious sanctions arising from its violation, can be employed as a bargaining tool to charge exorbitant fees to companies that seek to buy licenses to practice the patent."); and Broadcom Corp. v. Qualcomm Inc., 501 F.3d 297, 313-14 (3d Cir. 2007) (citing Daniel G. Swanson & William J. Baumol, Reasonable and Nondiscriminatory (RAND) Royalties, Standards Selection, and Control of Market Power, 73 ANTITRUST L.J. 1, 5, 10-11 (2005)) (commenting that lock-in creates the potential for anticompetitive effects and that "[i]t is in such circumstances that measures such as FRAND commitments become important safeguards against monopoly power").

[19] Apple, Inc., 2012 WL 2376664, at *12.

[20] Id. at *13 (citing eBay, 574 U.S. at 391-92).

[21] Id.

[22] Spansion, Inc. v. Int'l Trade Comm'n, 629 F.3d. 1331, 1359 (Fed. Cir. 2010) ("Given the different statutory underpinnings for relief before the Commission in Section 337 actions and before the district courts in suits for patent infringement, this court holds that eBay does not apply to Commission remedy determinations under Section 337.").

[23] Use of the ITC as a venue for patent challenges has tripled in the last ten years. Colleen V. Chien, Patently Protectionist? An Empirical Analysis of Patent Cases at the International Trade Commission, 50 WM. & MARY L. REV. 63, 68 (2008). Sixty-five percent of those cases proceed simultaneously in federal district court. Id. at 64. See also 2011 Report at 239-240 ("Expanded use of the ITC and the parallel proceedings in district courts have led some commentators to raise concerns about inconsistent results in individual cases and incoherent development of patent policy.").

[24] 19 U.S.C. § 1337(a)(1)(A)-(B).

[25] 19 U.S.C. § 1337(f).

[26] Limited exclusion orders block importation of infringing articles by "persons determined by the Commission to be violating" Section 337. General exclusion orders ban the importation of any infringing goods, but such orders are available only in narrow circumstances. 19 U.S.C. § 1337(d)(1), (2); Kyocera Wireless Corp. v. Int'l Trade Comm'n, 545 F.3d 1340, 1356-58 (Fed. Cir. 2008).

[27] 19 U.S.C. § 1337(d)(1).

[28] Our research has revealed only three cases in the past 35 years in which the ITC has denied an exclusion order on public interest grounds. Those cases involved issues of public health or broad public interest. See Certain Fluidized Supporting Apparatus, Inv. No. 337-TA-182/188 (1984) (holding that it was not in the public interest to exclude specialized hospital beds for burn patients, when the domestic producer could not supply alternative beds within a reasonable time); Certain Inclined-Field Acceleration Tubes, Inv. No. 337-TA-67 (1980) (citing overriding public interest in basic atomic research using imported acceleration tubes that were superior to the domestic alternative); Automatic Crankpin Grinders, Inv. No. 337-TA-60 (1979) (finding that it was not in the public interest during the energy crisis of the late 1970s to exclude an automobile engine component that improved fuel economy, when domestic industry was unable to meet domestic demand); Sapna Kumar, The Other Patent Agency: Congressional Regulation of the ITC, 61 FLA. L. REV. 529, 567-68 (2009). More recently, the ITC limited an exclusion order in a setting where exclusion would decrease the effectiveness of first responders during an emergency. Certain Baseband Processor Chips and Chipsets, Transmitter and Receiver (Radio) Chips, Power Control Chips, and Products Containing Same, including Cellular Telephone Handsets, Inv. No. 337-TA-543 (2007).

[29] Commentators have highlighted the need to harmonize the remedial standards in the two venues. See Robert W. Hahn & Hal J. Singer, Assessing Bias in Patent Infringement Cases: A Review of International Trade Commission Decisions, 21 HARV. J.L. & TECH. 457, 486-90 (2008); Kumar, supra note 19, at 574- 78.

[30] 19 U.S.C. § 1337(b)(2).

[31] The FTC did not take a position on the facts of the investigations, or whether the ITC should issue remedies. The FTC also did not address whether seeking an injunction or exclusion order for RAND-encumbered SEPs would violate Section 5 of the Federal Trade Commission Act, 15 U.S.C. § 45, or Sections 1 or 2 of the Sherman Act, 15 U.S.C. §§ 1-2.

[32] In its recent statement to the ITC, the FTC acknowledged that "the [ITC] has consistently held that the benefit of lower prices to consumers does not outweigh the benefit of providing

complainants with an effective remedy for an intellectual property-based Section 337 violation." Certain Digital Television Products and Certain Products Containing Same and Methods of Using Same, Inv. No. 337-TA-617, Comm'n Op. at 16 (Apr. 2009). See also 19 U.S.C. § 1337(d)(1), (f)(1).

[33] See 2003 Report at 223-28.

[34] Cf. 2011 Report at 234-35 ("A prior RAND commitment can provide strong evidence that denial of the injunction and ongoing royalties will not irreparably harm the patentee.").

[35] 19 U.S.C. § 1337(d)(1), (f)(1).

[36] See 2011 Report at 243 ("Assertion of a patent against a standard, especially a patent subject to a RAND commitment, creates a particularly important scenario for considering the public interest in deciding whether to grant an exclusion order" before the ITC).

[37] Certain Gaming and Entertainment Consoles, Related Software, and Components Thereof, Initial Determination at 300 (May 2012); see also id. at 303 ("[T]he evidence supports Microsoft's conclusion that Motorola was not interested in good faith negotiations and in extending a RAND license to it.").

[38] There is precedent for such an approach at the ITC. In December 2011, the ITC found that HTC infringed valid Apple patents. "Based on consideration of competitive conditions in the United States economy," the ITC delayed the effective date of the exclusion order for four months "to provide a transition period for U.S. carriers." Certain Personal Data and Mobile Communications Devices and Related Software, Notice of the Comm'n's Final Determination Finding a Violation of Section 337 at 3 (Dec. 2011).

[39] Certain Wireless Communication Devices, Portable Music and Data Processing Devices, Computers and Components Therof, Notice of Commission Decision to Review In Part A Final Initial Determination Finding a Violation of Section 337 at 4-5 (June 2012). Briefing by the parties on these questions is due on July 9, 2012. Id.

[40] Id.

In: Standard-Essential Patent Holders
Editors: R. B. Vega and M. Guzman ISBN: 978-1-62618-207-3

Chapter 6

INTELLECTUAL PROPERTY RIGHTS PROTECTION AND ENFORCEMENT: SECTION 337 OF THE TARIFF ACT OF 1930*

Shayerah Ilias

SUMMARY

Section 337 of the Tariff Act of 1930 allows U.S. companies to protect themselves from imports that infringe intellectual property rights. The U.S. International Trade Commission (ITC) adjudicates complaints filed by U.S. companies alleging Section 337 violations.

Primary remedies under Section 337 include exclusion orders and cease and desist orders. In recent years, there has been an increase in the number of Section 337 proceedings or actions. Members of Congress have expressed concern about the length of time for completion of Section 337 investigations and the effectiveness of enforcement of exclusion orders.

* This is an edited, reformatted and augmented version of a Congressional Research Service publication, CRS Report for Congress RS22880, prepared for Members and Committees of Congress, from www.crs.gov, dated October 26, 2009.

Section 337 of the Tariff Act of 1930

Section 337 of the Tariff Act of 1930 (19 U.S.C. §1337) is the primary option available to U.S. companies to protect themselves from imports into the United States of goods made by foreign companies that infringe U.S. intellectual property rights (IPR), such as patents, trademarks, and copyrights.[1]

The U.S. International Trade Commission (ITC) administers Section 337 investigations. The ITC is a quasi-judicial federal government agency responsible for investigating and arbitrating complaints of unfair trade practices. The majority of unfair competition acts asserted under Section 337 involve allegations of patent infringement. These cases tend to be complex and require adjudication by the ITC.[2] In the case of most copyrights and trademarks, the Department of Homeland Security's Customs and Border Protection (CBP) agency, is empowered to make on-the-spot determinations of IPR infringement.[3]

Requirements for Filing a Section 337 Complaint

In general, U.S. companies must fulfill three requirements in order to assert unfair competition under Section 337. First, there must be an importation or a sale for, sale after, or potential future importation of the infringing product into the United States. It is not necessary for the imports to be in commercial, or mass, quantities. Second, an unfair act of competition relating to the imported good must occur, i.e., an infringement of a valid U.S. patent, copyright, or trademark. Third, a domestic company must be engaged in sufficient domestic activity, such as investment in plant and equipment or employment of labor and capital, in the United States related to the imported product in question. U.S. citizenship is not necessary to meet this third requirement.[4]

Standard Section 337 ITC Investigations

Investigation Process

Under statute, Section 337 investigations must completed "at the earliest practicable time" (19 U.S.C. §1337). The ITC issues "target dates" for identifying when the ITC proceedings should be completed. Previously, the ITC has attempted to complete most investigations in less than 15 months. In recent years, the target dates for many investigations have increased, due in part to the growing complexity of the subject matter and number of unfair acts under investigation in cases and the workload of ITC judges.[5] As shown in *Table 1*, Section 337 ITC investigations involve multiple steps that take place over the course of many months.

Table 1. Summary of Section 337 Investigation Process

Action	Timetable
Complainant files Section 337 case	Start of investigation
Decision to institute Section 337 case	Within 30 days after filing of complaint
Target date set for completion of investigation	Within 45 days after publication of notice of investigation
Evidentiary hearing	Initial Determination must be issued at least four months before target date
Initial Determination	
Decision on whether to review Initial Determination	Within 45 days after Initial Determination issued
Final Determination	Issued by target date
Enforceability of ITC determination	Within 60 days, unless disapproved by the President for policy reasons

Filing a Section 337 Complaint

Any company seeking relief under Section 337 must prepare a detailed complaint with information supporting the claims with the ITC, including background information on the intellectual property asserted in the claim and evidence of infringement.[6]

Institution and Assignment of Case

Upon receiving a complaint, the ITC has thirty days to determine whether or not to initiate a Section 337 investigation. If an investigation is instituted, the ITC assigns the case to an Administrative Law Judge (ALJ), who oversees and conducts the investigation. The ITC also assigns an investigative attorney from its Office of Unfair Import Investigations (OUII), who provides his or her views to the ALJ regarding whether or not a Section 337 violation has taken place. The attorney also represents the public interest during the investigation. A target date for completion of the investigation will be set.

Evidentiary Hearing

The ALJ conducts a formal evidentiary hearing, typically lasting one to two weeks, generally within seven to ten months of the filing.

Initial Determination of Case

The ALJ then issues a preliminary ruling (an "Initial Determination") determining whether or not a Section 337 violation has occurred and proposing remedies (discussed in next section) if violations are found. The ALJ decision is based on the merits of the case. For instance, in a Section 337 case involving U.S. patents, the ALJ would evaluate the case based on patent infringement issues. The Initial Determination must be issued no later than four months prior to the target date.

Final Determination of Case

Within 45 days of the Initial Determination, the ITC Commissioners decide whether or not to review the Initial Determination. The Commissioners may decide to adopt the ruling. Alternately, they may elect to change all or some parts of the Initial Determination, or to completely reject or remand it. Generally, within three months of the Initial Determination, the Commissioners issue a "Final Determination," which takes into account public interest considerations, such as the impact on the public's health and safety or on the ability to satisfy U.S. market demands.

Settlement

Some cases before the ITC are settled before a final decision is made. Complainants (typically the patent holder) and respondents (the alleged infringer) may move to terminate an investigation. For instance, they may agree to cross-licensing or to resolve the dispute through arbitration.

Review of Determination

The Final Determination is sent to the President for review based on national security considerations. This decision is enforceable within 60 days if no actions are taken by the President. The President rarely has overturned the Final Determination. During the 60 day review period, respondents who continue activities ruled by the ITC to be in violation of Section 337 do so under bond. If the Final Determination is *not* disapproved by the President, respondents engaging in such activities stand to lose a significant amount of money. In some cases, the bond is 100% of the total value of the imported products. Thus, while remedies are not enforceable until the conclusion of the

60 day review period, the bond frequently serves as a deterrent from engaging in IPR-infringing activities. This is especially the case because the President rarely disapproves of ITC Final Determinations.

Appeals

Within the 60-day Presidential review period, the respondent (or anyone adversely affected by the Final Determination) can file an appeal of the decision to the U.S. Court of Appeals for the Federal Circuit. Depending on the circumstances, the Final Determination may or may not be enforceable while the appeal is being heard.

Amendments to Section 337

In the original enactment of Section 337, Congress stipulated that the ITC complete investigations within 15 months (from institution of a case to Final Determination). Section 337 was later amended to become compliant with the General Agreement on Tariffs and Trade (GATT), whose national treatment provision requires that member states not treat foreign member states' nationals any less favorably than their own nationals. There was concern that Section 337, as initially enacted, may not have allowed foreign companies to defend themselves adequately because the ITC adjudication process generally takes place at a faster pace than litigation in federal district courts. The ITC is now required by statute to complete investigations "at the earliest practicable time" (19 U.S.C §1337).

Section 337 Remedies and Enforcement

The ITC grants two primary remedies to U.S. companies: exclusion orders and cease and desist orders. The ITC may *not* issue monetary damages to U.S. companies. The time that it takes for remedies to become enforceable may vary because of differences in target dates and the possibility of appeals by respondents.

Exclusion Orders

Exclusion orders prohibit the importation of the infringing good into the United States. They are effective for as long as the patent is valid. Limited exclusion orders, the most commonly issued type of exclusion order, prohibit the importation of only those infringing goods originating from the parties named in the ITC investigation. In contrast, general exclusion orders prohibit the importation of *all* goods of the kind determined to be infringing, irrespective of the source of the infringing good. Because general exclusion orders are broad in their scope, they may disrupt international trade significantly. In general, they are issued only when circumvention of a limited exclusion order would be likely or it would be difficult to identify all infringing parties. The U.S. Customs and Border Protection agency enforces exclusion orders.

Cease and Desist Orders

Cease and desist orders require the termination of infringing-related activities, such as selling infringing articles previously imported that are currently in domestic inventories. These orders frequently are issued in conjunction with exclusion orders, particularly in situations where the infringing goods are imported in commercial quantities. Cease and desist orders are enforced by the ITC, which is authorized to impose civil penalties on U.S. importers that violate cease and desist orders. Penalties per day may be as high as $100,000 or double the value of the goods involved.[7]

PRELIMINARY RELIEF

U.S. companies may request that the ITC conduct expedited temporary relief proceedings and issue a temporary exclusion or cease and desist order while the regular investigation takes place. For preliminary relief, U.S. companies must provide significantly more evidence prior to the hearing than for a standard case. The ITC's decision to grant preliminary injunctions is based on: the likelihood of success for the complainant's case and the extent to which the domestic industry, respondents, and the public interest would be adversely affected if a preliminary injunction was not issued.

For temporary relief proceedings, a Final Determination (following an Initial Determination by the ALJ) is granted 90 days after institution for standard cases. For more complex cases, a Final Determination is granted 150 days after institution of the case. In cases where the complainant receives a temporary remedy, the complainant is required to put up a bond. Following the preliminary ruling, the full Section 337 standard case will proceed. If the preliminary injunction is not upheld in the regular investigation, the complainant may lose the bond money.

TRENDS IN SECTION 337 CASES

In FY2008, the ITC reported a total of 88 active Section 337 investigations and ancillary proceedings, up from 73 in FY2007. Of the 88 active investigations in FY2008, 43 represented new Section 337 investigations and 7 represented new ancillary proceedings stemming from previously concluded Section 337 investigations.[8] The Section 337 investigations frequently involved advanced technology areas such as integrated circuits, computer components, consumer electronic products, and chemical compositions. Over 90% of the new Section 337 investigations that were active in FY2008 involved cases of alleged patent infringement.[9]

Since 2002, there has been a general uptick in the number of Section 337 cases. In FY2008, the number of new cases was nearly four times higher than the number of new cases in FY2000. There also were over 50% more active cases in FY2008, compared to FY2007.[10] The overall rise in international IPR infringement has contributed to the increase in Section 337 activity. Additionally, there has been increased publicity of the ITC as an IPR border enforcement entity, partly due to recent high-profile rulings.[11] Moreover, there is greater corporate awareness of the potential benefits of filing a Section 337 case. Prior to 2006, the average length for investigations (in which a final decision was reached) was less than 15 months. In FY2008, the average length for investigations rose to 16.7 months; the shortest completion time was six months and the longest was 28 months.[12] In FY2008, the ITC issued two general exclusion orders, five limited exclusion orders, and 14 cease and desist orders.[13] In the prior year, the ITC issued four general exclusion orders, five limited exclusion order, and 14 cease and desist orders.[14]

ALTERNATIVE TO SECTION 337 INVESTIGATIONS

U.S. companies also may bring lawsuits against foreign entities in the venue of U.S. district courts to challenge the entry of infringing products into the United States. Federal district courts, unlike the ITC, can award monetary damages to the IPR holder and issue injunctions against infringers. If the adjudicated infringer violates the injunction by continuing to import the infringing product, it may face sanctions if the rights holder claims the infringer has acted in contempt of court. However, the federal courts do not possess direct authority to block imports, as the ability to issue exclusion orders enforced by the CBP rests with the ITC. If the adjudicated infringer lacks assets in the United States, enforcing a U.S. court's orders may prove difficult.[15]

In addition, litigation in U.S. district courts tends to be more costly and to take longer to yield decisions than the Section 337 venue.

Issues for Congress

Some Members of Congress have expressed concern that the Section 337 venue does not provide immediate relief to U.S. companies facing unfair import competition. Proponents of a faster process have argued that the U.S. economy and public health and safety may be adversely affected by the continued importation of IPR-infringing goods while Section 337 investigations take place.[16]

ITC proponents maintain that the length of time for investigations has risen because of increased Section 337 activity, which has contributed to heavier dockets for ALJs and investigation backlogs. In addition, they indicate that recent cases tend to involve more technologically complex products and that filings increasingly name multiple respondents, whereas previous cases generally named one respondent.[17] Others point out that ITC investigations are generally faster than litigation in federal district courts, where proceedings may take several years.

Concerns also have been raised about CBP enforcement of exclusion orders. A recent Government Accountability Office (GAO) report notes that U.S. companies spend millions of dollars to file Section 337 complaints before the ITC, but that enforcement of exclusion orders is limited because of a lack of resources. As of July 2007, CBP reported that 66 exclusion orders were in effect.

The number of exclusion order exams carried out by CBP has declined since FY2002. While U.S. capacity to carry out IPR enforcement has increased, according to GAO, challenges remain because IPR enforcement frequently may not be a top CBP priority and there may not be adequate resources targeted to this effort.[18]

End Notes

[1] For more information on IPR protection and enforcement, see CRS Report RL34292, Intellectual Property Rights and International Trade, by Shayerah Ilias and Ian F. Fergusson.

[2] Telephone conversation with ITC official, March 19, 2008.

[3] 19 U.S.C, § 156; 19 U.S.C. §1595a, and 19 C.F.R. §133.42.

[4] Thus, foreign companies with sufficient U.S. activity are able to file Section 337 complaints.

[5] ITC, Section 337 Investigations: Answers to Frequently Asked Questions, Publication No. 4105, March 2009, p. 23.

[6] For more information on filing a Section 337 complaint, see ITC, Section 337 Investigations: Answers to Frequently Asked Questions, Publication No. 4105, March 2009. 19 C.F.R. Part 210 discusses the ITC investigation process, time frame, and parties involved.

[7] Steven D. Hemminger, "Section 337 of the Tariff Act: Global IP Protection in Our Global Economy?," Intellectual Property & Technology Law Journal, Vol. 19, No. 4, April 2007.

[8] ITC, Year in Review: FY2008, USITC Publication No. 4093, p. 14. ITC, Year in Review: FY2007, USITC Publication No. 4002, p. 16.

[9] ITC, Year in Review: FY2008, USITC Publication No. 4093, p. 14.

[10] ITC, Performance and Accountability Report: FY2008, p. 73.

[11] For instance, in the 2007 Certain Baseband Processor Chips (337-TA-543) case, Broadcom obtained a limited exclusion order prohibiting Qualcomm from importing infringing chips.

[12] ITC, Performance and Accountability Report: FY2008, pp. 68, 71.

[13] ITC, Year in Review: Fiscal Year 2008, USITC Publication 4093, p. 14.

[14] ITC, Year in Review: Fiscal Year 2007, USITC Publication 4002, p. 16.

[15] Telephone conversation with USITC official, March 19, 2008.

[16] U.S. Congress, Senate Committee on Finance, Customs Reauthorization: Strengthening U.S. Economic Interests and Security , Testimony by Greg P. Brown, Counsel, Ford Global Technologies, 110th Cong., 2nd sess., March 13, 2008.

[17] Telephone conversation with ITC official, April 24, 2008.

[18] U.S. Government Accountability Office, Intellectual Property: Federal Enforcement Has Generally Increased, but Assessing Performance Could Strengthen Law Enforcement Efforts, GAO-08-157, March 2008.

In: Standard-Essential Patent Holders
Editors: R. B. Vega and M. Guzman
ISBN: 978-1-62618-207-3

Chapter 7

FACTS AND TRENDS REGARDING USITC SECTION 337 INVESTIGATIONS*

U.S. International Trade Commission

The U.S. International Trade Commission (USITC) adjudicates allegations of unfair acts in connection with imports under Section 337 of the Tariff Act of 1930 as amended, 19 U.S.C. § 1337. Most Section 337 investigations involve allegations of infringement of patents or other IP rights. Facts and trends regarding certain aspects of Section 337 proceedings are provided below.

1. INCREASED CASELOAD

The number of new Section 337 investigations has increased by over 530% from FY 2000 to FY 2011. New complaint filings in FY 2012 indicate that the active caseload will likely remain stable or increase in the current fiscal year. Given the USITC's speed and patent expertise, Section 337 proceedings involving high tech products, such as smartphones and tablet computers, account for an increased share of these investigations in recent years. Smartphone companies involved in Section 337 investigations during the first half of FY 2012 include: Apple (14), HTC (8), Motorola (4), Samsung (3), RIM (3), Nokia (3), and LG (1).

* This is an edited, reformatted and augmented version of a U.S. International Trade Commission publication, dated June 18, 2012.

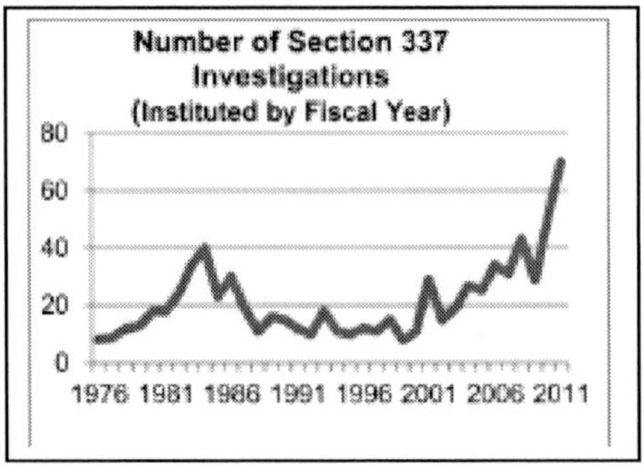

The USITC has taken steps to accommodate the burgeoning caseload including increased staffing for the Office of Administrative Law Judges and the General Counsel's Office. The USITC is also building a new courtroom for Section 337 proceedings that is expected to be completed by the fall of 2012. The USITC continues to focus its efforts on maintaining expeditious target dates for completion of its investigations.

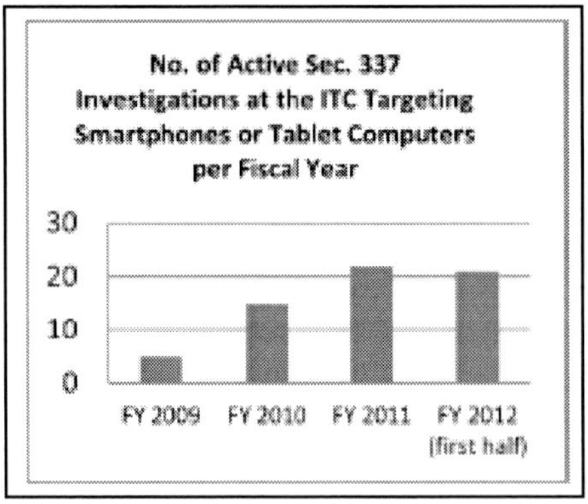

2. Domestic Industry Requirements and Non-Practicing Entities

An essential element of a Section 337 violation is the domestic industry requirement. This requirement may be met by showing that the complainant has made sufficient investments in the United States with respect to articles protected by the IP right concerned.

The statute was amended in 1988 to allow IP rights-holders that do not manufacture products (*i.e.*, non-practicing entities) to obtain remedies at the USITC. Congress made note in amending the statute that inventors, universities, start-ups, and other entities that conduct R&D, engineering, or licensing activities are equally entitled to Section 337 relief as are manufacturing industries. In fact, one of the motivations behind the amendments was to overturn the USITC's decision denying relief to a licensing entity, Warner Brothers, in connection with copyrighted Gremlins products because the USITC did not recognize licensing as a domestic industry.

An issue currently receiving attention is whether non-practicing entities (NPEs) should be permitted to obtain relief at the ITC. There is no commonly understood definition of an NPE. For analytical purposes, entities that do not manufacture a product that practices the specific patents asserted in a Section 337 complaint are referred to here as Category 1 NPEs. Category 1 NPEs include manufacturers whose products do not practice the asserted patents; inventors who may have done R&D or built prototypes, but do not make a product covered by the asserted patents and are therefore relying on licensing to meet the domestic industry requirement; research institutions, such as universities and laboratories, that do not make products covered by the patents, and therefore are relying on licensing to meet the domestic industry requirement; and start-ups that possess IP rights but do not yet manufacture a product that practices the patent. Another category of NPEs that do not manufacture products that practice the asserted patents, and whose business model primarily focuses on purchasing and asserting patents, are referred to here as Category 2 NPEs.

Some commentators have recently suggested that NPE filings, particularly by Category 2 NPEs, account for the increased caseload at the USITC, because of the U.S. Supreme Court's decision in *eBay v. MercExchange*. However, this suggestion does not appear to be supported by data concerning complaint filings at the USITC since the *eBay* decision was issued.

Data concerning NPE filings at the USITC show the following:

- Since the eBay decision on May 15, 2006, the USITC instituted 258 investigations through the first quarter of 2012. Of these, only 21 investigations (or 8%) involved complaints that were filed by Category 2 NPEs.
- Only one Category 2 NPE complainant was successful in obtaining an exclusion order – this was Rambus in Inv. No. 337-TA-661.

- Category 1 NPEs accounted for 26 investigations (or 10%) of the 258 investigations.
- Only two Category 1 NPEs were successful in obtaining an exclusion order – these were Tessera in Inv. No. 337-TA-605, and UNeMed Corporation, the technology transfer office of the University of Nebraska Medical Center, in Inv. No. 337-TA-679.

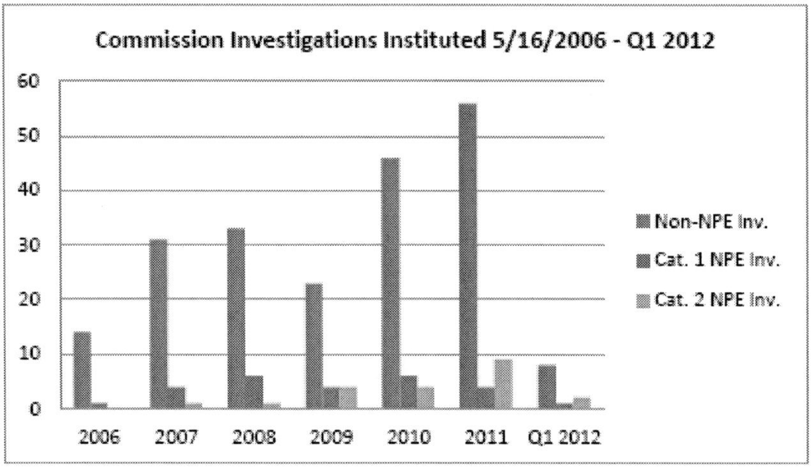

3. SETTLEMENTS

About half of all investigations instituted at the USITC ultimately terminate based on settlements or consent orders. It has been suggested by some commentators that NPEs file complaints at the USITC for the purpose of obtaining settlements. However, due to the relatively small number of NPE investigations, data concerning settlements are inconclusive.

Settlements (5/15/2006 to Q1 2012)			
	Number of Completed Inv.	Number of Settled Inv.	Settlement Rates
Total Inv.	196	97	49.49%
Cat. 1 NPEs	21	8	38.10%
Cat. 2 NPEs	13	8	61.54%
All NPEs	34	16	47.06%
All Other	162	82	50.62%

4. Number of Respondents

USITC jurisdiction and remedies are *in rem,* relating to the imported articles in issue. In 2008, the U.S. Court of Appeals for the Federal Circuit in *Kyocera v. Int'l Trade Comm'n,* rejected the USITC's long-standing practice of including within the scope of its remedial orders not only infringing components but also downstream products containing such components that were manufactured by third parties who were not named respondents in its investigations.

As a result of this decision, commentators have observed an increase in the number of respondents named in Section 337 investigations as complainants can no longer rely on the pre-*Kyocera* Commission practice to reach third party downstream products containing accused components.

Some commentators have suggested that the total number of respondents in NPE investigations has increased significantly. The data concerning respondents named in Section 337 investigations show that there is great variability in the numbers of respondents across all investigations. The table below shows the range of numbers of respondents named in USITC investigations.

In 2009, for example, investigations instituted based on complaints filed by Category 1 NPEs involved from 3 to 6 respondents; investigations instituted based on complaints filed by Category 2 NPEs involved from 10 to 16 respondents; and investigations instituted based on complaints filed by all other complainants involved from 1 to 22 respondents.

Range of Number of Respondents Investigations Instituted 5/16/2006 - Q1 2012			
YEAR	Category 1 NPEs	Category 2 NPEs	All Other
2006	4	0	(1-21)
2007	(2-7)	1	(1-46)
2008	(4-40)	18	(1-34)
2009	(3-6)	(10-16)	(1-22)
2010	(1-17)	(2-10)	(1-30)
2011	(4-49)	(4-33)	(1-39)
Q1 2012	35	(2-21)	(2-33)

Data concerning the total number of named respondents indicate that the number of respondents named in investigations varies substantially from year to year in each category of investigations.

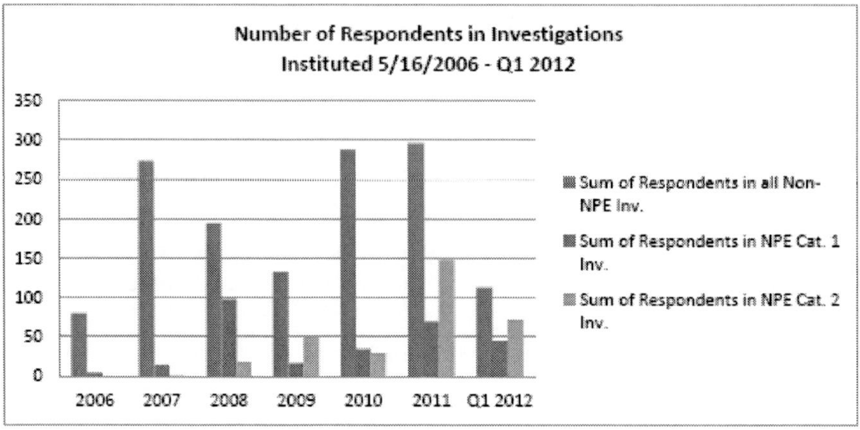
Number of Respondents in Investigations
Instituted 5/16/2006 - Q1 2012
350
300
250
200
150
100
50
0
2006
2007
2008
2009
2010
2011
Q1 2012
Sum of Respondents in all Non-NPE Inv.
Sum of Respondents in NPE Cat. 1 Inv.
Sum of Respondents in NPE Cat. 2 Inv.

INDEX

L

M

N

O

P

U

V

W

Y